BEAUTY BIAS

Discrimination and Social Power

Bonnie Berry

PRAEGER

Westport, Connecticut
London

Library of Congress Cataloging-in-Publication Data

Berry, Bonnie.
Beauty bias : discrimination and social power / Bonnie Berry
    p. cm.
   Includes bibliographical references and index.
   ISBN 978–0–275–99012–1 (alk. paper)
   1. Physical-appearance-based bias.   2. Beauty, Personal—Social aspects.
I. Title.
  HM1091.B47   2007
  306.4′613—dc22   2007014269

British Library Cataloguing in Publication Data is available.

Library of Congress Catalog Card Number: 2007014269
ISBN-13: 978–0–313–99012–1
ISBN-10: 0–313–99012–5

First published in 2007

Praeger Publishers, 88 Post Road West, Westport, CT 06881
An imprint of Greenwood Publishing Group, Inc.
www.praeger.com

Printed in the United States of America

The paper used in this book complies with the
Permanent Paper Standard issued by the National
Information Standards Organization (Z39.48–1984).

10 9 8 7 6 5 4 3 2 1

For Samantha Robichaud,
denied the American Dream

Contents

Preface   ix

1   Introduction: The Power of Looks   1

Part 1   The Ramifications   15

1   Looks and Health   17
2   Looks and Romance   29
3   Looks and the Workplace   39

Part 2   The Pressures   53

4   The Diet, Fitness, and Supplements Industries   55
5   Cosmetics, Cosmeceuticals, and Other Superficial Changes   63
6   The Plastic Surgery Industry   71

Part 3   The System   85

7   The Medical and Health Insurance Communities   87
8   The Legal Community   95
9   The Economy, Globalization, and Power   101
10   Conclusion: Toward an Acceptance of Looks Diversity   111

Appendixes
    Appendix A: Filmography   127
    Appendix B: Selected Resources   129

Notes   133

Bibliography   157

Subject Index   161

Name Index   163

Preface

This book is about bias. All societies exhibit bias, based on a variety of their populations' traits such as race, gender, age, economic resources, and physical ability. This book is about those traditional biases as well as the social inequality centered on physical appearance. Physical features such as skin color, hair texture, height, weight, eye shape, disabilities and deformities, condition of the teeth, evidence of aging, and "beauty" are important markers for biased treatment. Those of us with the "wrong" features, per societal-wide agreement, are subject to several forms of bias.

That is, physical features are the focal points, the means by which we admit or reject people from any number of social opportunities, such as employment, college admission, and romance. As I will detail throughout this book, what we look like influences greatly our access to jobs, romance, education, friendships, and (in short) all of the economic and more social network advantages that can be denied us or offered us.

Recently, it has been proposed in the media and elsewhere that prejudice and discrimination based on physical appearance is the last bastion of "socially acceptable" bias. To say that this form of bias is socially acceptable is not to say that it is okay or a good behavior and an appropriate perspective. It is merely to say that it is, for the most part, legal and ordinarily not met with strong personal rebuke, thus putting this form of bias at odds with the more traditional forms of bias (racism, etc.), which are not legal or publicly acceptable. For instance, passersby on the street can and often do make rude remarks to heavy people, and they do so without consequence.

Sometimes the bias we experience is blatant and sometimes it is subtle. In fact, we often are not told directly why we are rejected from a job or a club membership, when the reason is our physical appearance. At other times, appearance-bias is remarkably blunt, as we see in the astonishing "ugly laws" making it illegal for the disabled, maimed, deformed, and diseased to be abroad in the streets. You will read about these laws, in effect if not enforced, until the mid-1970s in the United States.

We can be equally astounded by the dangerous lengths to which we will go to be "beautiful." When we learn that a supermodel died after eating nothing for days and eating only lettuce and diet soda for months before, the power of social dictates to be thin is crystal clear.

Yet there is good news. Ugly laws do get repealed, largely because they were unenforceable and partly because of bystander outrage. After a few supermodels died in the quest for emaciation, a number of societies (Italy, India, Spain, and Britain) banned the too-thin ideal and now encourage a healthier model. Whether this move toward more generous sizes will filter down to broader society so that young women no longer starve themselves in search of social acceptance is as yet unknown. Also unknown but promising are the budding rights movements, such as the fat-acceptance movements, which emulate other, earlier minority rights movements. It was a long, difficult struggle for women, racial and ethnic minorities, the disabled, and the aged to gain a semblance of equality. But it is happening and is happening still, reliant upon the same principles (education, policy changes, and grassroots awareness) that are making it possible for lessened racism, sexism, ableism, and ageism and that could portend a remedy for appearance-bias.

Getting in the way of such change are lingering and highly resistant social attitudes about, for example, fault, blame, and personal responsibility. This topic will be much revisited in discussions of appearance. We assign blame to those with less than optimal appearance, as though they can force themselves to be more attractive if they tried. The fuller and more fact-based explanation is that much about our looks is only mildly within our control, subject to genetics, financial well being, and health. Another point of resistance is one that continually startled me whenever I came to grips with it during the course of writing this book: We are talking about *visible* traits, traits that have little or nothing to do with capability. Yet we use these visible signs as a *reason* for limiting social opportunities, no matter how nonsensical that is. It may be that we use these meaningless visible traits merely as a way to reduce the social competition, to keep our competitors to a minimum, much as we have traditionally with race and gender.

As expected, this work is grounded in historical accounts of social pressures to look a particular way (how appearance standards have and have not changed over time), the things we do to make ourselves more attractive (foot binding, cosmetics use, plastic surgery, and the like), and the many industries involved in the appearance phenomena. After the Introduction, in which I discuss the rudimentaries such as the subjectivity of beauty and the changing nature of what is considered attractive, the next three chapters in Part I explain the ways in which our physical appearance affects our health, our chances at romance (and marriage and family), and our workplace experience. With workplace experience, for example, we see the double standards imposed on women for their appearance that are not similarly imposed on men, in addition to the obvious cases of looks-based discrimination against the not-so-young, the nonwhite, and the disabled.

Part II describes the activities that we undergo in order to be more socially desirable via our appearance: the ingestion of vitamins, supplements, steroids, and growth hormones; the diets we undertake; the cosmetics we apply, the cosmeceuticals we use, and the plastic surgery that we increasingly undergo. These industries, as I call them, not surprisingly function on a capitalist model, encouraging us to buy the goods and services that promise (and often fail) to make us attractive, while they also encourage us to accept ourselves "as is" if that is also profitable (by providing plus-size clothing, for instance).

Part III informs us of the "system." The system comprises the medical and health insurance communities, the legal community, and the global and economic community, and these communities respond to us differentially, depending upon what we look like. These communities can redress our grievances of discrimination via legal actions, offer or refuse health care depending upon our appearance, and exploit our anxieties to match an increasingly global and homogenized standard of beauty.

Having addressed these topics, in the Conclusion I bring home a final and crucial point, well founded in the feminist perspective: *choice* to engage in appearance-enhancement is key. At this final juncture, I also twist the foregoing issues around and look at them inside out, where possible; for example, I will discuss an anti-thin bias and bias against the beautiful. My main point here is the reminder that physical features are artificial markers, with meaning only as attached by society; meaning: no features are superior or inferior innately. More broadly, the small but incremental strides we have made toward appearance-acceptance are described and likened to other minority rights movements. Having described the social forces involved in these changes (the media and education), I then examine the legislative, policy, and grassroots efforts that challenge the appearance-bias landscape. This leaves us to ponder whether there will come a time when, as whole societies, we accept people as equal regardless of appearance, whether we are tall, blonde, and with attractive European features or whether we are, as are most of us, plain.

I come to this stage in my work, quite logically, after a career-long interest in social inequality. My previous work has concentrated on the disparity between how we treat people based on their economic status (such as the biases evident in crime control as directed against the poor, primarily imprisonment), gender, race, and sexual orientation. Less obviously but still very much to do with inequality, I have compared social attitudes about and treatment of nonhuman animals to our attitudes about and treatment of humans, and found the attitudes and treatment leveled against nonhumans and human minorities remarkably similar. In a way, the project about which you are to read observes a new and yet not-so-new form of social bias. Certainly we have long (always?) imposed appearance standards on others and had those standards imposed on us. But we haven't studied it as thoroughly as we might have, until now.

At the completion of this work, I am grateful for the advice and support of many, many people. Among them are friends and colleagues who have served as enormous resources, some of whom have reviewed my work as it progressed and all of whom have shared helpful ideas: Joanne Belknap of the University of Colorado, Earl Smith of Wake Forest University, Susan Schweik of the University of California at Berkeley, Karlene Faith of Simon Fraser University, Paul Longmore of San Francisco State University, Hugo Freund of Union College, Rosemary Erickson of Athena Research Center, Prabha Unnithan of Colorado State University, and an anonymous reviewer. I would also have been lost without the expert and patient assistance of my editor, Hilary Claggett of Praeger/Greenwood. Professional organizations have provided fora for this work to be presented to fellow social scientists, namely the Society for the Study of Social Problems and the Association for Humanist Sociology. My family, especially my sisters Sharon and Ruth and my niece Sarah, have calmly listened to my whining about the lack of fun time. Not to be dismissed, my cats, Misery, Blue, and Skippy, have provided much needed amusement, comfort, and kindness. Finally and most importantly, I am more-than-can-be-expressed grateful to Peter Lara, my partner and best friend.

Introduction:
The Power of Looks

Waiting for the oil to be changed in my car, I wandered across the street
and into a greeting card shop. There I saw a number of cards for all occasions, with pictorial illustrations and with varying messages and sentiments.
Among them were birthday cards with cartoon-drawn and photographed
pictures of old people, highlighting the sagginess of their bodies, with sexual invitations as the intended joke. Other birthday cards showed photos
of an unattractive old woman with loose lips and apparently no teeth, and
a very old man with similar features, inviting the recipient of the card to
be kissed. Still other cards featured massive women offering themselves,
sexually, as birthday presents. As illustrated by these cards, it is assumed
that no one would want to have sexual or romantic encounters with such
people. These cards, for sale in an ordinary card shop, also clearly suggest that it is acceptable to make fun of people with undesirable physical
features. It is barely imaginable today that a commercially successful card
shop would display blatantly anti-Semitic, racist, or sexist greeting cards.
Deriding people, based on their physical appearance, is the "last taboo."
Only now, in the twenty-first century, are we developing an inkling that
such behavior bespeaks bias.[1]

These cards remind me of other messages that we see in our daily lives.
A magazine advertisement lists sights that the magazine reader would
presumably find repulsive, including "Roadkill" and other negative images,
but also "Fat Guys in Speedos."[2] A magazine story about college life shows
a photo of a frat boy wearing a T-shirt stating, "Freshman girls. Get 'em

while they're skinny."[3] In a mall parking lot, I saw a bumper sticker that read: "BEER: helping ugly people have sex since 1862."[4] And there are the license plate holders that read, "No Fat Chicks."

It is not illegal to display such messages. Seeing and displaying derogatory messages about people's physical appearance are not something that we even think about, usually. It is as though unattractive and (I will argue) ordinary-looking people are fair game for insults and, as we shall see, discrimination. Just as we have struggled with sexism and racism in our society—the prejudice and discrimination against women and nonwhites—bias exacts economic and other (more purely social) tolls on the nonbeautiful. As with race and gender, our physical features are mostly beyond our control: most of us cannot help what we look like any more than we can influence the race and gender we are born into. And, although most of us are not beautiful, beautiful people are the standard by which we are compared. This fact alone begs important questions about unattainable expectations and curious social rewards and punishments, based on our looks.

In *The Beauty Myth*, Naomi Wolf describes the "ideal" woman as "tall, thin, white, and blond, a face without pores, asymmetry, or flaws, someone wholly 'perfect.'"[5] These "ideals" serve a function, Wolf explains, and the purpose is an economic one; a purpose that will be evident throughout this book. In Wolf's terms, the unrealistic expectations to be beautiful that we (women especially but men increasingly so, as I will describe) all face increase profits for advertisers and the media, the same entities that create the "ideal" in the first place.[6] This feedback loop reinforces the "ideal," making it seem (because we see it repeatedly in advertising and in the media) as though the "ideal" is somehow valid. Wolf also claims that the beauty ideal serves a political end in that, "the stronger women became politically, the heavier the ideals of beauty would bear down on them, mostly in order to distract their energy and undermine their progress."[7] That is, the criteria for beauty shift and become more stringent, making beauty more and more unreachable, setting the boundaries for beauty farther beyond the horizon than most of us can achieve; and these shifting criteria serve even more so as a way to control women.

Subjectivity

Beauty is in the eye of the beholder, it has long been said, implying that beauty is subjective. It has also long been said that beauty is as beauty does, implying that we can and ought to enhance our looks to their optimum potential. In fact, beauty is defined socially and is very much agreed upon. Moreover, beauty is mostly a matter of genetics and subject to alteration only to a small degree. Also, beauty isn't all there is to the social acceptability of looks. Height, skin color, hair texture, eye shape, etc.—along with the ambiguously defined "beauty"—influence the social power that we possess or are deprived of possessing, including the jobs we get, the salaries we earn, the clubs we join, the people we marry, the friendships we make, and the colleges we enter.

The reader is well aware that what is considered attractive changes over time and varies across cultures. The fact that our standards change (as discussed below) tells us of their subjectivity. On the historical dimension, we once revered plumpness and now we don't. On the geographical dimension, a few cultures admire teeth sharpened to points as a sign of beauty, but most don't. Some cultures elongate the neck by encircling it with brass rings, insert lip plates, and paint their teeth as signs of beauty.[8] Other cultures seek out women for features that we in the West would dislike, such as droopy breasts.[9] In other words, the dominant culture in any society determines what good looks are and are not. Yet, amazingly, and especially as time progresses, there appears to be quite a bit of agreement about attractiveness.[10] Probably the best explanation for this consensus is globalization. Through TV, movies, advertisements, and other visual media, our standards of acceptable and unacceptable looks have homogenized. Northern European standards of attractiveness apply across all societies, including African and Asian ones, such that tall, slender, white, blonde, light-eyed, and flowing-haired features are the standards against which we are all judged. These features are represented on billboards and by department store mannequins, around the world.[11]

On the whole, symmetry of facial features and a healthy appearance (versus a diseased or sickly one) are universal signs of physically acceptable looks, if not beauty.[12] Although there are microcosms that deviate from universal standards (and admire sharpened teeth and the like), mostly the standards apply cross-culturally. People agree about what constitutes a beautiful face, finding similar features (such as large eyes and narrow noses) "universal features of beauty." Even ethnic groups who do not share such features as narrow noses consider such features attractive.[13]

*Un*attractiveness is also uncertainly subjective, although we think we know it when we see it. One of the reasons for the decline of "ugly law" was this fact of ambiguity about ugliness. "Ugly laws" were in effect in several cities (San Francisco, Chicago, Denver, Columbus, and others) from the years 1867 to 1974. They were aimed at keeping "unsightly beggars" off the streets and out of public view, with penalties including fines and incarceration. But what constitutes ugliness? The ordinances specified lists of traits, namely evidence of disease, mutilation, maiming, and deformities.[14] Clearly, these features pertain to physical disabilities rather than ugliness as we commonly think of it.

The disabled, though not necessarily unattractive, are often objectified, depersonalized, and assumed, *because* of their disability, to be unattractive, and they experience some of the same bias (employment and other) as the unattractive. Deformities, especially highly visible facial-cranial deformities, are real enough and unambiguous in their consequences, as we shall see in the chapter on looks and the workplace. Facial deformities, probably because they are so visible, "have a profoundly disenfranchising effect on people, more so than disabling conditions such as blindness or a missing limb."[15] A psychiatrist remarks, "If people are deformed, they may be converted into *things*, and treated in an altered manner. The *contents* of an individual who is visibly marred are devalued, and the person has to struggle to avoid being discredited as an object. . . . The very beautiful are also converted into *objects* by onlookers, but they do not share the negative or frightening tone set by deformity."[16] So the beautiful and the nonbeautiful can both be objectified, but the nonbeautiful more negatively so.

This book is not about beauty so much as it is about nonbeauty and the social reaction to that. We are judged on our weight, our age, our skin color, and all of our physical traits. We often do not measure up and thus our access to economic and social opportunities are negatively influenced by our appearance. This is not to say that plain-looking and unattractive people are completely denied opportunities. Of course most of us find employment, love, and friendship. The argument here is that the plain and unattractive are less likely than the attractive to have equal access to top-choice jobs, romance, friendships, club memberships, and so on. Oddly, even beautiful people fail to measure up in all contexts, as when the bar is set super-model high, or, less commonly, in those rare circumstances when beauty is a disadvantage.

Implying that appearance is subjective and that we constantly compare ourselves to others, Charles Darwin wrote, "If every one were cast in the same mold there would be no such thing as beauty."[17] In other words, if we all looked the same, there would be no such phenomena as those about which I discuss in this book. We tend to measure ourselves against others and this phenomenon is a social one rather than an innate one, meaning that we are socialized to engage in these judgments. These social judgments about our looks raise the intriguing question of why, as whole societies, we set appearance standards, as seemingly inarguable criteria, which restrict equal access to social power. Perhaps we do this because physical appearance is visible and thus easy to make judgments about. The essence of this point about judgment, though, is the meaninglessness of the judgment. At its very basis, appearance, like gender and race, has nothing to do with the capabilities of a person.

The Changing Nature of the Meaning of Looks

The social values placed on looks change, and the fact that they do tells us something very important about their meaninglessness. Of course the social values placed on appearance are meaningful in their *consequences*; that is what this book is about. What I mean is that physical features themselves are meaningless until meaning is attached to them. For instance, bias against Asian eye shapes, dark (nonwhite) skin, and Negroid hair texture are mere overlays. There is nothing inherently good or bad about these features. The features themselves are neutral except for the meanings attributed to them, changeable though these meanings may be.

And change they do. Thin lips, thick lips. Tan skin, pale skin. Curly hair, straight hair. Corpulent bodies, thin bodies. They have all been valued and devalued over time.

If we compare our beauty ideals over the past century, just on body size alone, we find that the tide turned in the 1890s when we began to devalue fleshy bodies. With a few, short-lived exceptions, such as the 1950s when our icons such as Marilyn Monroe and Jayne Mansfield were fat by today's standards and circa 1990 when Madonna exemplified the muscular ideal, we have valued the thin body. Through the 1920s (recall the flat-chested, thin flapper), the 1960s (think Twiggy, the famous very thin British model), and onward, we have admired and hoped to emulate the very thin body.

Currently, in most societies, obesity is a scourge to be avoided at all cost. It wasn't always that way as we know from Western art, notably the work of Rubens as illustrated by his "Rubenesque" bodies, indicating that plumpness was fashionable into the nineteenth century as a sign of beauty for women, and prosperity and good health for men. That changed in the 1890s, and henceforward there grew a powerful stigma against fat bodies.[18] Within subcultures, there may be different views of obesity and, to make matters more complex, these views may be dependent upon economic conditions. For instance, African American males and females have long had a more positive perspective on obesity than American whites. But, as African Americans became more middle class, their perspectives on obesity changed to more closely approximate those of whites.

Furthermore, consider the changing nature of the health-looks nexus. In April of 2005, it was reported that being overweight (excluding morbid obesity) is actually healthier than being thin. Specifically, it was reported that people who are moderately overweight live longer than people who are not overweight.[19] This finding has already been disputed but, if verified, the finding would be a delight to the majority of Americans who are overweight. It does not mean, even if verified, that the stigma against large body mass will dissipate. Stigma, it can be predicted, will continue against people-of-size even if they are seen as healthy. Health is one issue, looks are quite another.

Partly, our fluctuations in beauty standards are the result of fluctuations in our feelings about morality, health, wealth, and racism. We expect moral, healthy, prosperous, and socially accepted people to appear a particular way. For instance, to be broadly racially acceptable to all groups, minority and majority, African Americans have been encouraged, even intraracially, to not look "too Black."[20] Less so during the Black power ("Black is Beautiful") movement of the 1970s, but for the most part, it has been unpopular, socially and within the African American community, to have strong ethnic features. Thus, African Americans have undergone the surgeries and the sometimes-dangerous cosmetic treatments (such as lip thinning, rhinoplasty, and skin lightening) to appear more Caucasian. Similar patterns are found to be true for Asians, Jews, and other ethnic groups who have their facial features altered in the direction of whiteness, as shown in Chapters 5 and 6 on cosmetics and plastic surgery. As usual, the impetus is socioeconomic success.

Other examples of acceptable physical appearances fitting with social statements about people, as though one's physical appearance designates or serves as a sign of social acceptability, are size (related to economic status) and evidence of disease (related to immoral behavior). Financially sound people presently (but not historically) are, on the whole, thinner than poor people.[21] From the literature on size, we repeatedly find arguments pairing corpulence and immorality, a lack of self-control, and a "flawed character."[22] Before advanced treatment of sexually transmitted diseases, we found morality interacting with the aesthetic concerns of the "syphilitic nose." Such a nose was considered a definite sign of decadence, one we would go to surgical extremes (rebuilding the nose) to rid ourselves of as an obvious sign of immorality.[23]

The overall pattern of changing expectations cited in literature on the topic and in the media is that our expectations have evolved toward greater rigidity. In the past thirty to forty years, our ideals of human, especially women's, bodies have diverged from physical reality. Decades ago, fashion models weighed less than average American women, but only by about 8 percent. Later, in the 1990s, models weighed 23 percent less than average women, suggesting that our ideals (as judged by fashion models) have become unrealistically thin over the past four decades.[24] We have become broadly rigid, unsparingly so, in terms of our homogenized, globalized, and unreachable (for most of us) expectations that we all appear as flawless ideals of the tall, thin, blonde beauty.

Terminology

To allay any confusion about the words and phrases used in this book, let us at the outset consider terminology. Most if not all descriptors of physical appearance, such as "good looks," "ugly," "attractive," and "unattractive" are ambiguous and unmeasured. They cannot be clarified in any meaningful and useful way since, apart from the homogenization, globalization, and universalism arguments about beauty, the dimensions of beauty and non-beauty are not quantifiable and not entirely agreed upon. We may agree that thin hair is less attractive than thick hair, that wrinkles are less preferable than smooth skin, and so on. We may agree about these things, even though they may or may not have much personal meaning for us in terms of how we feel about people whom we know, and whom we like, who have thin hair and wrinkles. On a societal-wide level, however, "unattractive" features may stand in the way of being asked for a date or being hired for a job. And in that sense, since these features have real consequences, we can describe them as "unattractive," if for no other reason than to say that, societally, we agree that thin hair and wrinkles are not desirable traits.

Since looks are a social phenomenon, we could substitute "socially desirable" and "socially acceptable" for the commonly used terms "attractive," "unattractive," etc., to indicate that which is *socially dictated* as desirable and acceptable, at that historical moment. Conversely, "socially undesirable" and "socially unacceptable" refer to looks that society has determined to be devalued. Having pointed out the enormous role that society plays in determining what is attractive and not attractive, I have elected to not use this cumbersome language throughout the book. Sure, it sounds more politically correct to add "socially" in front of an adjective about physical appearance. And yes, I want to avoid using words that will insult anyone. However, I think it best to admit that we all have a fairly good, if inexact, idea about what the common terms ("attractive," etc.) mean. Rife with social bias, desirable and acceptable looks mean all the things we know them to mean: straight and white teeth, youthful and clear skin, taut muscles, clear eyes, and so on.

Size Terminology

Terms like "standard" or "medium," when referring to those not "overweight" are misleading since a majority of the U.S. population (and growing proportions in other populations) are "overweight." Standards about body mass change over time, as best illustrated by insurance corporations' weight charts for healthy and unhealthy weight/height ratios.[25] But as Marilyn Wann, a leading figure in the fat-acceptance movement aptly notes, these health insurance and medical standards are arbitrary. In the late 1990s, the federal government "adopted new, lower cutoff points for 'overweight' and 'obesity.' The result: ninety-seven million Americans —or fifty percent of us—are now fat. On the day *before* the government's ruling, only fifty-eight million people, or one-third of us, were fat."[26] This changing definition of what constitutes too-much weight will be discussed in depth in the chapter on medical and health insurance communities (Chapter 7). The change occurred, as we will discover, largely at the behest of insurance corporations, which establish the weight charts. Their reason for changing the weight charts (mainly reducing the amount of acceptable and insurable weight levels) was and is to reduce their risk of insuring those with obesity-related illnesses; correspondingly, the charts allowed the insurers to deny coverage to heavier people or to increase premiums for heavier people. Weight standards are not only arbitrary and fluctuating, they also vary across genders as well, with women-of-size facing less leeway in additional pounds and greater bias than men-of-size.

Specific to body size terminology, I will use a variety of terms, such as "heavy," "people-of-size," and "overweight" to refer to those who are heavy. The term "heavy" is useful because it refers merely to pounds. Pounds weigh something, thus a person weighing 300 pounds is heavier than a person weighing 140 pounds.

The word "fat" has great utility as well, and the fat-acceptance movement encourages the use of the word "fat" instead of "obese," "overweight," and other "polite" terms for large body mass. As discussed by fat-acceptance advocates, the term "overweight" implies an abnormality. To wit, the person who is overweight weighs *too much*. Too much for what? For her own good? To be aesthetically pleasing to the public?[27] Wann encourages the use of "fat" as a descriptor since, she points out, there is nothing wrong with being fat. It is just as polite to say "fat," she writes, as it is to say "young" or "tall" and, I would add, "white," "immigrant," "woman," and other social-placing descriptors.[28] Agreeing with Wann, Sondra Solovay, a lawyer specializing in legal issues surrounding fat acceptance, prefers the word "fat" to "overweight" and "obese" because "overweight" assumes an ideal weight and "obese" is a "loaded, medical determination." As to the latter, "obese" and "obesity" are used in medical contexts, and fat, according to the fat-acceptance advocates, has nothing to do with the health of a person.[29] However, the use of the word "fat" is not well-received by all, and many find the term insulting.

Looks Bias: How and Why It Operates

Bias against people based on their physical appearance can operate alone as a looks-based stigma or it can reinforce other "ism's," such as racism, sexism, ageism, ableism, and classism. Usually, looksism is hidden and unknown, not unlike sexism and other ism's, such that the victim may not be given the true explanation for unequal treatment. Although, and this is an important point, occasionally we *are* told that we are rejected from a job (or a friendship or a date) because of our looks. When this happens, it is a clear indication that the rejecters think that physical appearance is a sufficient and appropriate reason for rejecting people based on their looks. More often than not, though, we are given an explanation much more palatable and much less sue-able, such as, "You're just not as qualified as the other applicants." To date, looks-bias is largely anecdotal. To some extent it is unmeasured because, as just mentioned, we are not told the real reasons for denial of employment, health care, housing, friendships, dates, and so on: mostly, the deniers (landlords, health insurers, and employers) are not going to freely and openly admit to their prejudices and their discriminatory practices. Nonetheless, there is some documentation that I will supply, showing comparative rates of looks-biased treatment. When we reflect upon it, bias *is* clear in a number of social contexts, from disparities in salaries, to airplane seating, to the higher prices charged for plus-sized clothing.

Looks-based prejudice is as baseless and absurd as other prejudices. We commonly hear it said that size bias is an appropriate criterion for refusing someone a job, as in, "Well, he should lose weight if he wants a better job." This implies two things. First, it implies that weight loss is within the person's control, while there is abundant evidence that it is not. Second, it implies that a heavy person *cannot* do the job. In sum, the argument goes, not only *ought* heavy people lose weight in order to be socially acceptable but it is a matter of job capability as well. We also hear it said that a person cannot have or keep a job in the public eye because of a deformity or aging. Deformities, aging, and other appearance traits have nothing to do with the ability to serve as counterhelp, restaurant manager, or any other work role. I will offer a number of real-life examples of the poor fit between appearance and presumed incapability.

It has further been offered that, not only is looks bias reasonable and appropriate, but there is a positive economic function to discriminating against people based on their looks. The clothier Abercrombie and Fitch seems to believe that attractive, young, white models and sales staff are crucial to their profits. And, although they are subject to legal action, as will be discussed in Chapter 3 (on looks and the workplace), they are not alone in feeling that way. Most advertisements utilize attractive people to enhance the sale of products and services. Bias in this form serves corporate needs, if not the needs of individuals or society.

Judging people based on physical appearance serves a stratifying function. If there is nothing inherently good or bad about being attractive or unattractive, as I have argued, the question then becomes why looks-stratification exists and why it continues. To accept or exclude people, to place them in hierarchies with this placement then determining life chances regarding income/jobs, marriages/social networks, and so on, purposely maintains an uneven playing field. The purpose of an uneven playing field, looks-wise, is the same as the purpose of an uneven playing field based on sexism, racism, ageism, and other ism's: Such bias benefits *some* to the detriment of many. Those with power (notably employers, media, advertisers, educational institutions, and policymakers) determine who has access to power, ensuring that those in power maintain undiluted power. Sexism and racism long prevented women and nonwhites from getting traditionally white male jobs (as professors, doctors, airline pilots, and the like) and thus kept competition at a minimum, among white men only.[30] To level the playing fields, as we progressively have done with the women's movement and the civil rights movement, it had to be made clear that women and minorities are as capable as men and whites. In leveling the looks-based playing field, the trick will be to redefine human worth based on something other than looks.

In essence, the possible purpose and certain consequences of looks bias are to draw distinctions between people, based on their looks, regardless of how artificial those distinctions are. The purpose of *that* is twofold. There is the monetary purpose, for instance to sell extra airplane seats to those who fill more than a single seat. And there is an attributional purpose, meaning that discrimination is thought to reflect well on the discriminator. For example, if Abercrombie and Fitch hires only young, beautiful, northern European-featured models and sales staff, the thinking goes, then Abercrombie and Fitch must be a "successful" and "superior" company, since the people representing them have "successful" and "superior" traits.

Changing Ourselves, Changing the World

There are two basic avenues that humans can pursue to equalize our place in looks-rankings. We can alter our appearance (the traditional response) and we can try to alter the way society views and treats us, based on our appearance.

The Things We Do for Looks

Some of us respond to pressures to be attractive, to be as presentable as possible, in simple, temporary, and commonplace ways. We diet, exercise, take supplements, apply make-up, and color our hair. An increasingly common response is plastic surgery, a more dangerous, expensive, and life-threatening remedy. Much of what we do to alter our appearances (from hair straighteners to plastic surgery) has to do with blending in, with homogenizing ourselves to a global ideal. In present-day Japan and Vietnam, skin-lightening, nose-lengthening, and eye-reshaping are methods by which to assimilate Euro-American standards of beauty.[31] Africans in Africa and African Americans whiten their skin, at some danger to themselves, in order to enhance their social status and gain access to power through marriage and jobs. A minority of Chinese have undergone leg-lengthening surgery for the same reasons. The same would be true for nose jobs to alter the "Irish nose" and the "Jewish nose." But a part of blending in also means trying to be beautiful and thin because, while most of us are not beautiful and thin, the standards to be so are ubiquitous.

Activism and the Redefinition of Looks

Alternatively, a very different reaction only recently taking hold, is defiance of societal demands to look a particular way. In this approach, we find a growing body of policy changes, social movements, and organizations constituting a refusal to go along with such social dictates, in the hope instead of advancing acceptance of those of us who are not "ideal." The fat-acceptance movement, for example, like other human rights movements, attempts to not only raise awareness but also to make concrete legal changes, such as expanding rights to health care, physical access, and equal employment.[32] Unfortunately, there is no such organization as of yet in support of people with other stigmatized traits, such as the deformed and the unattractive. We need, and I hope to offer, a better understanding of why this is so. One explanation is that unattractiveness is more subjective and thus difficult to measure, while height and weight are measurable, thus making size-related equality movements more successful. Another explanation is that unattractive people are *so* (self- and other-) stigmatized that fear of derision may prohibit their asking for recognition and equal treatment.

Conclusion

This story is not without irony. Most of us are not especially attractive, but we are under social pressure to be so. And most of us succumb to this pressure; we try to be as attractive and as socially appealing as possible. This fact alone, that most of us are not beautiful, makes quizzical the employment, dating and marriage, and other life-altering judgments about our looks. Although most of us do what we can to make ourselves presentable, there is a limit to what we can do to alter our appearance. Yet we are encouraged (expected?) to be beautiful, and that is the standard by which we are judged.

Where we go from here is a journey through the many ways in which we, as members of the public, are affected by public reaction to our physical appearance. Together, let us examine the physical features themselves, such as hair texture, skin color, and body mass in association with other traits such as race, gender, age, health, abled-ness, and social class. In the first section, health, romance, and workplace issues, as they pertain to appearance, are addressed. Then we contemplate the things we do to alter our appearance, from the temporary and inexpensive (diet, drugs, cosmetics, and cosmeceuticals) to the permanent, expensive, and dangerous (surgery). Following that, we investigate the legal, medical, and economic industries involved. For example, our profit-oriented economic system influences how we respond to pressures to be acceptable by offering us (for instance) diet books and diet pills at the same time as we are offered large-sized clothing—leaving us to wonder if we should strive to be thin or to proudly accept our size no matter how massive. Finally, we encounter a new view of the future and how attitudes may change toward a more egalitarian approach to looks-diversity. Throughout, my intention is to raise new questions, and turn entrenched assumptions upside down and view them from a different angle, to better understand this important social phenomenon.

This examination has opened my eyes to a new way of looking at inequality. I hope the reader finds the study as insightful and as enjoyable to read, as I did in researching it.

PART 1

The Ramifications

CHAPTER 1

Looks and Health

Here, and in the chapters on plastic surgery and on nonsurgical means of appearance-alteration (diets, supplements, exercise, and vitamin use), I will address health-and-appearance issues relevant to our dissatisfaction with our looks, often fed by public perception about our appearance. Although this book covers a wide array of physical features as focal points subject to bias or admiration (skin color, height, hair texture, etc.), this chapter will concentrate on body weight, since much of the looks-health controversy is about weight.

After a brief introduction to the relative importance of looks *versus* health, which will include a discussion on disability and looks, I will cover the disagreement over whether being overweight is a healthy condition or an unhealthy condition, the latter being the traditional view. Following that, special attention will be paid to the increasing number of children-of-size. Then I will direct the focus to the unresolved question of *deservingness*: whether people can control their weight or whether their weight is more the fault of biology (genetics and race) or an obesity-encouraging environment. Conclusions about blame, choice, and deservingness, if they fall on the side of individual freedom of choice to be overweight, overlap with other socially condemnatory "fault" assumptions such as the ill effects of smoking and drinking. Finally, I discuss *acceptance* and *normalization* of obesity: whether such acceptance encourages obesity and whether that is a problem. It seems that we, as a society, are in the midst of reconstructing our views on body size. Underlying this reconstruction are social agendas, such as the obvious medical agenda to alarm us about the health hazards of increased weight versus the far less obvious profit-oriented agenda to encourage size acceptance.

Health versus Looks

Relying on anthropological, psychological, and (less so) sociological studies, Nancy Etcoff describes the evolutionary forces in the social phenomenon of beauty. Basically, we assess people's presumed health and vitality based on youthful and attractive physical traits. All the visible signs of beauty, such as plentiful hair, unmarred skin, strong teeth, good musculature, upright posture, and a free-swinging gait speak to the health of an individual. From these cues, we make assumptions about fecundity. In other words, beauty, as an indicator of health is also an indicator of the ability to produce viable offspring. Beautiful people, the evolutionary argument goes, have long been and still are sought as breeding partners.[1]

When we turn to the question of health *versus* looks, things get a bit complicated. As you will read later, we often engage in practices that may not be healthy in order to be more physically acceptable, as when we undergo surgery, whiten our skin, or ingest growth hormones. For the moment, though, let's consider the motivation for some of these practices, which I will argue is more akin to beauty than health. Most of us watch our diets less out of concern for our health than for "the purpose of constructing hard bodies," and this motivation is as true for men as it is for women.[2] We know that, on the whole, women are more subject than men to the "tyranny of slenderness" and are more likely to engage in dangerous behaviors associated with anorexia nervosa, even though men are increasingly matching women on concerns about weight and willingness to engage in size-reducing activities.[3] We also know that when surveyed, many people report that they would rather have cancer than be fat. In short, looks trumps health as the *reason* for engaging in looks-enhancing behaviors.

Whether or not there are health disadvantages to being overweight, as described below, public reaction to being the "wrong" size can be unpleasant (in terms of social interaction) and costly (in terms of salary disparities and health insurance premiums). Since this is the case, "wanting to look good can be an even greater motivation than wanting to avoid chronic disease years down the line."[4]

Disabilities and Looks

We will learn more about the juncture between disability and looks, largely in terms of discrimination against the differently abled, in the chapter on workplace and in the chapter on the legal community.[5] Here, let me reiterate Etcoff's point that beauty is often equated with health. Clear eyes, clear skin, straight posture, good teeth, and in general an absence of physical defects are usually interpreted not only as signs of health but of beauty.

Note that the above-mentioned traits are *visible* indicators of health. Visible signs of beauty (health) are what this book is about: what the eyes tell us about people, often wrongly, are strictly visual cues. I asked Paul Longmore, an expert on disability, about the role that physical appearance plays in the social isolation of the disabled. Going on the assumption that much of the initial public negative reaction to disability is due to the visible signs of disability (wheelchairs and other accoutrements, unusual gait, missing limbs, prostheses, uncontrolled facial grimacing, etc.), I further assumed that invisible disabilities do not result in social prejudice and isolation. He affirmed that I was correct in guessing that invisible disabilities (asthma, chronic fatigue syndrome, deafness, heart and other internal organ conditions, and sometimes blindness) do not generate the same social stigma. He also pointed out that most (70 percent) of people with disabilities have nonapparent disabilities (learning disabilities, many psychiatric disabilities, mild cognitive disabilities, epilepsy, diabetes, arthritis, and so on) that become known only under certain circumstances, such as disclosure. Disclosure, he reminded me, triggers discrimination.[6]

The differently abled are, on the whole, marginalized because of their disability. They experience economic deprivation, with poverty rates ranging from 50 percent to 300 percent greater than the population at large. They are far more likely to be unemployed, to the tune of five times the national average; and they are paid about 20 percent less than abled workers, if they do have jobs. They are less likely to finish high school or college. They are socially isolated, being far less likely to go to restaurants, movies, concerts, sporting events, church, or go shopping. They are twice as likely than the abled to live alone; they marry later if at all, and are viewed as asexual.[7]

Perhaps in rebuttal to prejudice against the physically different, we have developed beauty contests limited to the disabled. Janeal Lee of Wisconsin received the "Ms. Wheelchair" prize in 2005. She was later denied the title when spotted standing in public. She has muscular dystrophy and can stand for brief periods.[8] Wendy Caldwell, who reported on this contest snafu, writes insightfully:

> Now, I've never been too fond of beauty pageants in the first place, but if there's one thing I dislike more than a beauty pageant, it's one that promotes any stereotype, especially one that people with disabilities are decidedly "different" than people without physical disabilities. According to this logic, Lee is too disabled to compete for the Miss Wisconsin title but not disabled enough to hold the Ms. Wheelchair Wisconsin title. Whether or nor Lee deserved to be discrowned is a moot point. Having separate pageants is a much larger abomination. By holding different pageants, we're telling people that those confined to wheelchairs are inherently different, not just in the manner of physical ability. It is our responsibility to help eliminate these generalizations by treating everyone as equals, especially in the instance of pageants.

This criticism brings up an excellent point: Should we and can we compare the physically different to the physically ordinary? Is there any chance that the differently abled can compare admirably to the abled (the physically ordinary)? Consider the one very significant factor visited above: the visibility of the difference. A deaf woman, Heather Whitestone, won the Miss America contest in 1995. She could physically perform all the tasks of the contest and she looked similarly beautiful to the other contestants.[9] Yet health differences, be they illnesses or merely differences (such as deafness), set distinctions between the disabled and not disabled. Socially, it helps to have an invisible rather than visible disability.

It's Not the Fat, It's the Fitness

An emerging perspective on the size-health exchange, one that has gained a lot of traction recently, is one suggesting that size is irrelevant to health. While experts disagree, one expert on physical activity remarks, "The impression is that everyone who is overweight faces an elevated risk for mortality. That's simply not true." Fat-and-fit proponents argue that we concentrate too little on exercise, eating well, and being physically fit while concentrating too much on being thin. Some people are simply born to be heavy, they argue, which does not mean they have health problems, especially if they exercise regularly and eat well. These people can be "obese" at the same time that they are metabolically healthy; they may, in fact, be built to carry a lot of weight and not suffer deleterious effects. In short, the fat-and-fit proposition presumes that any increased health risks associated with being heavy are the result of unhealthy habits, such as eating a poor diet and not exercising.[10] Moreover, it is unclear whether weight *loss* will prevent or decrease health problems (for example, whether weight loss is relevant to the risk of heart attack or stroke) or make us less likely to be hospitalized.[11]

Our societal emphasis on size is misleading in that thinness is considered a guarantor of health, when it is known that thin people can, of course, be unhealthy. It is true that those who are lean *and* active have the lowest mortality of all (compared to thin and inactive, heavy and inactive, and heavy and active), and to be both lean and fit is the optimal state. It has been proposed that one can be thin *or* heavy *and* be healthy so long as one is fit.[12] Although some experts say that the death rate for the thin-but-unfit is at least twice as high as those who are fat-and-fit, not everyone agrees. Heavy and fit women, for instance, have a similar risk of early death as unfit, thin women.[13]

Paul Campos, author of a book denouncing the "obesity myth," says that size "really doesn't matter. You can be just as healthy if you're fat as you can if you're slender."[14] Although he concentrates on the health questions related to size, coming down on the side of size being irrelevant to health, an equally important and underlying rationale, he says, for the United States obsession with weight is mostly found in "elite" Americans. Thinness, he writes, has metaphorical significance in the United States. Elites value thinness as a measure of morality and self-discipline, and thus it is viewed as a sign of moral character if we do not give in to desire. As many others have pointed out, a thin body signals a triumph of the will over our baser instincts.[15]

Indeed, according to some, not only is it okay to be fat, it is advantageous; if not regarding looks and social acceptance, then regarding health. A study published in 2005 gave temporary relief to concerned overweight people in the United States, showing that there are advantages to being moderately (but not greatly) overweight. "People who are overweight but not obese have a lower risk of death than those of normal weight," according to the National Cancer Institute and the Centers for Disease Control and Prevention.[16] The new study declares that obesity risks are and have been overstated and that pronounced thinness was related to "a slight increase in the risk of death."[17]

However, an analysis of these latest studies published in the *Journal of the American Medical Association* leaves us with a "perplexing message."[18] First of all, we must bear in mind that the new Centers for Disease Control and

Prevention (CDCP) study looked only at death rates and does not address the impact of excess weight on developing diabetes and other ailments that are clearly unhealthy. Instead, the 2005 study demonstrates that being heavy, especially in an extreme way, can be lethal. It is only when the benefits of being modestly overweight are factored in with extreme weight that we find mortality to be much smaller than previously thought. To muddy the waters further, in late 2006 we come back to the traditional viewpoint that being even moderately heavy can have a negative impact on health. The latest word is that "even a few extra pounds" may shorten lifespans.[19]

The Fat-Is-Not-Healthy Argument

Some people drink large quantities of alcohol over long periods of time and never develop drinking-related medical conditions. Some people smoke tobacco from their youth until their death at a ripe age from nontobacco-related causes, while others who have never smoked die of lung cancer. Some people engage in anorexic and bulimic behaviors and, if kept to a minimum, do not sicken and die from eating-disorder conditions. With other anorexics and bulimics, their eating patterns prove fatal. Some people are heavy most or all of their lives and exhibit no weight-related medical problems. Yet, we know empirically, documented in well-conducted science that there is a relationship, albeit a nonperfect one, between these behaviors (drinking, smoking, starving, and being overweight) and health problems.

For all the news about obesity not being such a bad thing health-wise, there remains a plenitude of data suggesting that it is. Most studies of health and size indicate that being heavy is related to cancer, heart problems, diabetes, hypertension, and other serious ailments. By the mid-1990s, we were discovering severe medical problems due to obesity: childhood Type 2 diabetes, a disturbing rate of a brain tumor-like condition among heavy women (pseudotumor cerebri), sleep apnea, hypertension, arthritis of the knee, etc. It is probably unhealthy to be obese, even if that means (as the fat-acceptance advocates say) that heavy people are reluctant to receive medical treatment. Yes, we should change our views on size such that heavy people do not face discrimination on health insurance, health care, employment, or any other measure. To deny, though, that there is any substance to the argument that weight is unrelated to health is not helpful. After all, we know that anorexia and bulimia, resulting in underweight, are unhealthy and even deadly.

However, to state categorically that fat itself *necessarily* causes health problems requires more convincing evidence than is currently available. While not entirely conclusive, it may very well be (as the fitness experts in the above section point out) that poor diet and lack of fitness cause the health problems rather than the fat itself.[20] Moreover, the health risks are not spread evenly across the population, partly because obesity is not spread evenly across the population, with the poor being overrepresented among the obese and the poor having little or no health care. And in the United States, racial and ethnic minorities are overly represented among the poor, uninsured, and unhealthy. "In the late twentieth-century America, it was the poor, the underserved, and the underrepresented who were most at risk from excess fat."[21] The health risks of being heavy, in other words, are greatly influenced by financial wellbeing.

Special Concerns about Children-of-Size

Children, worldwide, are growing heavier. Even in places one wouldn't expect, such as Asia, where healthy (low-fat, soy-based) eating habits and thin bodies have long been the tradition, we find an increasing number of heavy children. U.S. children particularly, are becoming "supersized," with more than one-fifth of preschool children being overweight and one out of ten considered "clinically obese." The explanations lie largely in the lack of physical activity and in the availability and abundance of fast food.[22] However, genetics, often overlapping with ethnicity, also play an important role: within the medical community it is thought that most heavy people, despite efforts to lose weight, inherit genes that keep them heavy (discussed below in the section on Choice).[23]

Of the growing number of heavy children in the United States (11.4 percent of elementary school children aged from 6 to 11), Mexican-American children are the most affected, with about 17.7 percent of Mexican-American children being overweight. Moreover, as a doctor who treats overweight children remarked, 10 to 15 years ago, those seeking treatment for their weight were 40 percent overweight, compared to now when they are about 80 percent overweight. This doctor went on to say that the public opinion of what is overweight has changed, to be more forgiving or generous, which may encourage obesity and may prevent weight loss.[24]

These children-of-size are succumbing to adult illnesses and middle-age health woes when they are still children, such as Type 2 diabetes, which has nearly doubled in 20 year's time, and was once thought to affect only older adults. Rates of gallbladder disease in children have tripled, and sleep apnea has increased fivefold.[25] Children in the United States, Britain, Spain, and Italy are growing heavy and thus experiencing the corresponding health problems of "metabolic syndrome": increased high blood pressure, raised cholesterol levels, and poor blood sugar regulation.[26]

Deservingness and Choice

Later, in the final chapter and elsewhere, I will address whether or not we *should* make ourselves as attractive as possible. It is known that well-groomed people are better received socially. It is also understood that we go to some lengths to make ourselves presentable, for instance, some of us color our gray hair, have weight-loss surgery, apply cosmetics, and ingest diet pills and growth hormones. At the moment, let's discuss the choice, if there is one, to lose weight or to not lose weight. In this context, let us consider social views on deservingness, specifically, whether society is correct to blame the weighty for their weight.

Weight-loss is not easy; some would argue, impossible. Certainly, the statistics on successful weight loss are disheartening. Medical studies find that if patients can lose weight, almost one-third of them regain it in a year's time and two-thirds regain it in 3 years. In 5 years, 80 to 90 percent regain the weight they lost.[27] Heavy people know they are reviled by society. They are blamed for not only their size (the thinking being that they should exercise more self-control) but also for increased health insurance premiums for all and, now, global warming (it takes more gasoline to transport heavier people). One would think, logically, that these social attitudes would make them do everything possible to lose weight. But it's not like quitting smoking. Many smokers stop smoking, successfully. The success rate for weight loss is far less impressive due to a number of factors beyond their personal control.[28]

Partly, we have an "obesogenic" environment to blame. An obesogenic environment speaks greatly to the type of and accessibility of food in the United States and elsewhere. Large portion sizes, fast food, and the ingredients of prepared foods (palm oil and high fructose corn syrup, notably) are part of this environment and are largely to blame for our increase in size over the past few decades. Our societal weight gain, according to experts on the subject, is environmentally induced in that a greater number of Americans are responding to a society that insidiously encourages them to be as heavy as their genetics allow them to be.[29]

Couple the obesogenic environment in combination with social class and ethnicity and we find multiple and additive influences on weight gain. Poor people and Hispanics are more prone to obesity for reasons of opportunity, values, and anthropology. As to opportunity and values, poor people have far less access to spas and gyms and even the rudimentaries like safe places to walk. The poor reportedly also do not to have an interest in exercising or watching their diets. Anthropologically, Mexican-Americans, long used to a starvation or near-starvation diet, developed the "thrifty gene." They, and other cultures used to a less-than-plentiful diet, developed a metabolism that very efficiently stores what little fat they can accumulate. When Mexicans arrive in the United States, where high-fat food is plentiful, the fat they ingest is proficiently stored; thus they gain weight more than people who are used to a more abundant diet.[30] Aside from environment, weight is sometimes associated with factors inarguably beyond our control, such as genetics, race, and class. For instance, up to 80 percent of obesity cases are genetically predisposed. People born to a heavy parent or two heavy parents are more likely to be heavy themselves. Even here, there is room for discrepancy such that children of heavy parents are not necessarily heavy themselves. We can only speak of *propensities* to be thin or heavy.

None of these factors provide the wholesale answer to what makes people heavy. Genetic predisposition, like an obesogenic environment and like ethnicity, can more accurately be understood as increasing the *likelihood* of weightiness. We know that size 0 models as well as a lot of thin people live in our obesogenic environment. And we know that there are plenty of thin Mexican-Americans, perhaps genetically predisposed and living in an obesogenic environment. Thus, we cannot blame obesity entirely on the environment.

We also know that, environmental influences cannot be denied as affecting the size of whole populations. Although measures of obesity vary over time (more on this in the chapter on health insurance and medical communities), no matter how obesity is measured and no matter the artificiality of its social meaning, people have become heavier in recent, obesogenic times. Nor can we dismiss, entirely, the genetic component. When doctors ask patients if there is a history of any particular disease (heart ailments, colon cancer, and so on) in the family, the doctor is expressing a documented viewpoint that genetics play a role in medical conditions (and many other characteristics) even if genetics *don't determine them.*

Blame for being heavy is commonly laid at the doorstep of heavy people, as a choice made to not exercise restraint. While the high-fat content of our food has an enormous impact on our increasing body size, Greg Critser suggests that we simply eat too much. We eat more than we need, we eat larger portions than in previous eras, we snack more, and we eat high-caloric convenience food. This eating pattern, Critser finds, is a post-1970s phenomena, and he convincingly argues that the phenomena has resulted from the profit motive. In the chapter on the economy (Chapter 9), I will offer a more elaborate discussion of capitalist influences on physical appearance, such as but not exclusive to cheaply manufactured food.[31]

Without getting into the fat content of food, Jean Renfro Anspaugh agrees with Critser that increased weight is the fault of excess food intake, and that one's weight is voluntary. Her insightful book on the diet culture, concentrating on the famous "Rice Diet," maintains that people are fat because they (including herself) eat too much.[32]

Yet, medical studies have also demonstrated that heavy people do not necessarily eat very much or that they eat no more than thin people. Moreover, we know that some thin people eat a great deal.[33] Approaching our next topic, acceptance versus rejection of size-diversity, Charisse Goodman writes, "one of the arguments promulgated by weight bigots is that since fat people have all gotten themselves into their predicament, they are not entitled to expect equitable, or even decent, treatment. Weight bigots employ this argument as a powerful lever to rationalize their prejudice." Size-ists, according to Goodman, believe that heavy people have *chosen* to look the way they do. As a consequence, society is justified in treating them with bias.[34]

Goodman is very likely correct in her conclusions. If so, the fat-revulsion prevalent in modern societies prevents at least some heavy people from seeking preventive and corrective medical attention out of fear of humiliation. Put another way, even if heavy people are heavy by choice—they eat a lot and don't work out—it still would be healthier for society and for the heavy people in it, were we to adopt a science-based, nonprejudicial view on size.

Construction and Reconstruction of Health and Looks

Clearly, social standards on what we should look like persist and these standards visit themselves upon us in very real and destructive ways. As we will see in the following chapters, we may be denied jobs or promotions because of what we look like, as well as access to other forms of social power (marriage, friendships, and so on).

Even if there has been a reevaluation of what constitutes unhealthy weight, especially in light of the new studies showing that being moderately overweight can be healthy, I think we will still find that the reevaluation is limited to health issues rather than beauty issues. As long as that is the case, obesity will receive its share of social bias.[35]

Historically, we have changed our minds about the meaning of body size, with the fleshy body once being seen as a sign of health and success in ages past, but now the fleshy body is something to be avoided at all cost.[36] The desirable, erotic body "is always a healthy body, even though the meaning of 'health' will also change."[37] It is unknown whether we in the near future will look upon the fat body as not only healthy but erotic, even though that is not the case at the moment. Certainly, there is a movement in that direction, as brought forward in the fat-is-beautiful movement described in the final chapter.[38]

Our social views of ideal body size have changed. We construct a social perspective of what is an attractive healthy body, using criteria such as weight, and we reconstruct that perspective by changing the criteria (great weight is attractive at times and lesser weight is attractive at other times). Constructions and reconstructions of body-size ideals do not exist on their own but instead are influenced by medical and economic views. Braziel and Le Besco's book, *Bodies out of Bounds*, serves to reconceptualize and reconfigure "corpulence." Specifically, they find that corpulence is not only historically, politically, and culturally constructed, but is also medically and economically constructed.[39] Medically, obesity is viewed as a primary source of medical problems such as hypertension, gallbladder disease, cancer, and cardiovascular disease. This medical interpretation is bound to the assumption that obesity itself is a preventable "disease" even though it is more accurately the symptoms (of diabetes, etc.) that evidence disease. This medical distinction, arbitrary though it is, may be more financially than medically determined, since "the possibility of prevention suggests a potential market."[40] In other words, there is a great deal of money to be made in selling medical remedies for obesity (diet pills, surgery, etc.) and its symptoms (medicine for diabetes, etc.). The medical community has a vested interest in viewing body size as changeable, as mutable, and the cures as viable.

Body size has a very complicated relationship to health, more so than is generally acknowledged. We have seen in this chapter that new studies and new views, such as the fat-and-fit perspective, question the health risk posed by body fat. Though there are some specific health risks associated with fatness, being heavy is not "the universally unhealthy condition that it is usually represented to be."[41]

Acceptance and Normalization

Some of us don't care what we look like and are unconcerned about size-related health. According to a survey on the topic, many overweight, out-of-shape "couch potatoes" are unconcerned about their size. Some of the respondents (12 percent) "pride themselves on not falling for the fitness craze." One explanation is that larger sizes are not only the current norm but are the *accepted* norm. Though most Americans are overweight and sedentary, they aren't bothered by it since they see so many other people who are similarly overweight and inactive.[42] Another measure of size-acceptance is the revision of medical and professional exercise prescriptions to be "more realistic" and "user-friendly" (read: easier).[43] Likewise, the CDCP came under "tremendous pressure to come up with more palatable recommendations" for exercise, otherwise people would not follow the regimens because they were "overly demanding."[44]

Plus, while thin bodies are still the ideal, we have developed a more relaxed attitude toward size-diversity, according to a survey conducted by NPD Group, a market research firm. Perhaps the respondents were merely being politically correct in their survey responses (not wanting to appear size-ist), or, perhaps given the portion of overweight people in our society, it is likely that many of the respondents were overweight themselves. Whatever the explanation, since the 1990s fewer people find overweight people unattractive.[45]

Normalization and acceptance is a topic to which I will return throughout this book. As we shall see later, the offering of plus-size services and products (furniture, coffins, seatbelt extenders, clothes, resorts, etc.) are strong indicators that large bodies are becoming very, very acceptable.

CHAPTER 2

Looks and Romance

This chapter will go beyond romance to discuss marriage and family, with romance usually being the precursor to committed relationships. We know that looks matter a great deal in dating, whether or not we can even get dates, and who we can get to date us. Looks also matter in family relations as we shall see, with our behavior toward our children dependent upon the children's physical appearance. But let's not get ahead of ourselves. First, let's talk about romance and dating.

In Jean Renfro Anspaugh's dead-on honest account of a live-in diet center in Durham, North Carolina, she recalls talking with another dieter about self-presentation in the context of dating. In recounting a date, the woman told Anspaugh about arranging her body on the couch so that the cellulite didn't show. Anspaugh, a heavy woman herself, knew immediately what she meant.[1] Most of us engage in impression management in some form, for romantic and many other purposes, from body posture to lip gloss to hair transplants.

Romance is important to most of us, regardless of sexual orientation or intended outcomes (marriage, sexual activity, etc.), and most of us want to have romantic partners. This is no less true of common-looking and unattractive people as it is for beautiful people. It's just that attractive people have more luck. "I would never have a boyfriend . . . , no one would ever love me in that way. . . . I was never going to have love."[2] This was written by Lucy Grealy, who as a small child had cancer of the jaw, causing part of her jaw to be removed, and leaving her with a facial difference that affected her self-image for the rest of her life. This passage was written of her adolescence, a year away from puberty. In fact, she had many lovers in her adult lifetime. And, in fact, she was not an unattractive woman, her deformity notwithstanding.[3]

In general, good-looking people fare better in the dating and marriage markets. Attractive people have the "capital" (their looks) to buy into many advantageous romantic relationships. It is well known that attractive women "marry up," which means, they marry men with more prestigious occupations and greater income than they themselves possess. It is also commonly known that attractive women and men are more popular with the opposite sex than are plain women and men, and that they, more than plain people, can have their pick of romantic partners. The physically attractive have more dates and more opportunities for sex.[4]

This pattern applies cross-culturally. Based on studies involving thousands of people and tens of cultures, appearance matters in mate selection. So does kindness and health but, across the board, physical appearance is in the top ten list of reasons for mate selection, with men valuing looks more than women.[5] The importance men place on looks applies across orientation: in personal ads, gay men and straight women (people seeking men) advertise their looks. Same-sex male relationships indicate that male interest in an attractive partner "is not just men's way of objectifying and denigrating women. Men interested in men are just as interested in the beauty and youth of their male partners."[6]

Explanations for Partner Selection

There are at least two reasons for appearance-based romantic choices. Besides the functionalist reasons, best put forward in evolutionary terms, there are social or marriage-market reasons, often having to do with financial power, which I will explain in a moment as attribution and social exchange.

Functional Explanations

To put it functionally, we are talking about mate selection, with mate selection not necessarily implying breeding potential, since mate selection can refer to selecting a person of the same gender, which, biologically speaking, has little to do with mating in its technical meaning. Plenty of heterosexuals may likewise not choose their mates for breeding purposes, although their choices may still be based on physical appearance. For those interested in breeding, however, looks-based selection explains the search for attractive breeding material and, in this case, can be discussed as an evolutionary force. At any rate, we often choose (unwisely) to date and marry the best-looking person we can get. Why do we do this?

Since humans have existed, the best evidence shows that we choose our mates on physical features, as illustrated by Nancy Etcoff's book *Survival of the Prettiest*. We have chosen them for indicators of health and fecundity (the ability to breed and to successfully produce healthy offspring). So we look for upright and straight posture, absence of physical impairments, clear eyes, good teeth, disease-free skin, significant height, etc. Additionally, and later in our human history, we focused on more minute beauty-related rather than health-related physical aspects like small waists on women. You get the idea: since recorded history, we choose, when possible, mates who look healthy and pretty.[7] That rules out the diseased, the differently abled, and the old. With age, for example, it is commonly understood (whether or not it's true) that women beyond a certain age are not healthy breeding stock. This age factor may still be operating today to rule out women over the age of 30 from getting lead romantic acting roles or from being the top choice for dates even among much older men.

From a functional interpretation, all this makes sense. Yet, one cannot help but wonder: if we choose our mates based on beauty, how is it possible that there are plain-looking people today? Using a strict evolutionary model, the plain and unattractive should have been bred out of existence in a natural selection process. Well, obviously, not all of us can attract beautiful mates. In fact, most of us can't and we have to settle for what we can get. Nevertheless, we still revere the beautiful and hold them up as ideal mating material.

Social-Market Explanations

As to present-day marriage-market reasons for choosing attractive partners, men who are not good-looking but are financially endowed may choose to marry the best-looking women they can afford, while less well-heeled women may choose to marry the most financially endowed men they can attract. Of course, it can happen in the reverse where wealthy, unattractive women attract young, attractive, not financially endowed men. But this arrangement occurs less often, since men have greater economic power, on the whole, than women. Regardless of the gender-power arrangement, the trade-off is money for beauty.

Consider celebrity cases in which older, unattractive, comb-over men with enormous monetary resources attract young, gorgeous women to marry them. To adopt a generous viewpoint, perhaps these beautiful women truly love these powerful men and would date and marry them even if they had no money, although such scenarios defy the popular imagination. The basic principle applies even to those of us who are not celebrities, residing in the everyday straits. Such arrangements are about power, with one person exchanging appearance (one form of power) for financial or other power. Let me now specify in greater detail, to explain the looks-based marriage-market using two theories: (a) social exchange and (b) attribution.

In sociological terms, we can address the appearance and romance nexus through our desire to be romantically associated with attractive people partly because, societally, we attribute positive traits to them and we can accrue social power merely by being associated with them. *Social exchange theory* is just what it sounds like. We view others in terms of what they can offer us. I go to the grocery store and give my money to the cashier and she lets me walk out of the store with a cartload of food. We talk to our friends on the telephone and, if all goes well, the conversation is friendly and supportive on both sides. Students pay university fees and gain knowledge and a college degree, while the professors earn a paycheck. Those of us who are not so attractive may attract romantic partners who are attractive because we possess a great personality or, more likely, a sturdy bank account, as illustrated above in the example of the unattractive and wealthy selecting and being selected by attractive and not-so-wealthy mates.

Attribution theory has long served as an explanation for why we favor attractive people. We attribute, erroneously, certain (positive and negative) psychological, physical, and personality traits to certain physical features. An example that comes swiftly to mind is "dumb blondes," in which we associate blonde hair with a lack of mental acuity. Attributions can be more positive as when we associate tallness with capability, or beauty with goodness. Social psychological studies have repeatedly shown that, in experiments in which respondents are asked to assign traits to photographs of people, they respond with a belief that attractive people are nicer, smarter, and better people, people that they would like to be with. Attribution reveals itself concretely in the social contexts of work, romance, education, sports activities, and so on. As I will demonstrate later, tall people are more likely to be hired for better positions and better pay, than short people. Heavy people are denied educational opportunities more than the ideal-sized. Short children are discriminated against in athletic events. And attractive people are sought after for romance, dating, and marriage.

Fitting social exchange and attribution theories together for the topic at hand, we now have an answer to the question of why we choose attractive people as our partners. We do so because they *reflect* well on us.[8] To have attractive partners says something positive about us. It says that we must have something to offer, especially if we ourselves are not attractive, if we have such attractive partners. Having an attractive partner is a sign of social power. If our good-looking partners have all these wonderful traits that we attribute to good-looking people (intelligence, personality, social power, sexual prowess, etc.), and they are associated with us in a romantic way, we are worthy.

Specific Physical Features' Effects on Romance Markets

Let us consider some of the features that we look for in our romantic partners. Youth, of course, is a premium: many of the signs of beauty have to do with youth/youthful appearance and, thus, mate selection.[9] Height is another such feature, with too much height not paying off for women but tallness being a desirable trait among men. Although, the tall-woman disadvantage is changing a bit over time, with tallness no longer being the social handicap it once was. Perhaps this is because many of the famous female beauties are tall, with the average fashion model being just over 5 feet and 9 inches.[10] Or perhaps it is because women have gained more, albeit not enough, social power. One wonders what this says about nonfamous tall women, who may still be at a major disadvantage in seeking romantic male partners of equal or greater height; clearly they face a smaller pool of men than do shorter women. One might also question why women are expected to be shorter than their male partners. The answer likely lies in social power differentials: women are "supposed to be" less powerful (shorter) than men.

The literature on physical appearance is replete with stories and research findings about the effect of girth, as another measure of size, on romance. In one study, researchers placed two bogus personal ads, one by a woman described as a drug addict, and one by a woman described as 50 pounds overweight. The ad by the supposed drug addict received 79 percent of the responses. In another study it was found that, of a sample of 10,000 people in their early 20s, heavy men were 11 percent and heavy women 20 percent less likely to be married than their thinner counterparts.[11]

Women bear the brunt of size prejudice, as witnessed by the massive research on the topic. The United States, from the 1920s to the 1960s, experienced what is called the "misogynist phase" with a "fat-refusal" movement focusing "primarily, and often nastily, on American women."[12] During this time, overt attention was placed on weight as the new gender divide, and has not let up since.[13]

On the other hand, the National Association to Advance Fat Acceptance (NAAFA) finds, based on anecdotal evidence, that 5 to 10 percent of the population prefer a heavy sexual partner.[14] These "fat admirers" (almost all of them men) attend NAAFA social gatherings in the hope of striking up romances with the heavy attendees (mostly women). Not surprisingly, the NAAFA women feel that they are valued solely for their appearance, for being heavy in this case, and resent the fat admirers' objectification of their body size. They complain, understandably, that the fat admirers are attracted to their size to the neglect of their intellectual and emotional traits.[15] Moreover, and in a way substantiating the objectification of their size, "it is the fattest of the NAAFA women who are most highly prized and sought after" by the fat admirers.[16] So here we have an organization, the NAAFA, which hopes to alleviate prejudice against the overweight, and of overweight women specifically, unintentionally creating an environment for sexual objectification of heavy women. The women in NAAFA want romantic involvement, but they want to be romanced for themselves, not for what they look like.[17] It seems antiegalitarian to use any physical attribute as an attractor *or* a detractor. To use either criterion in seeking romantic and sexual partners, thinness as an attractive trait or heaviness as a repugnant trait, seems artificial and superficial. Realizing that what one looks like *does* make a difference, we can only say that, in an egalitarian world, it would not matter what one looks like in order to have romance, a good job, or any access to a fulfilling life.

Skin color plays a large role, even within one race. Edwards, Carter-Tellison, and Herring, in their work on skin color and marital success, write of the enormous advantages that come with lighter skin tone among African Americans. Lighter skin color is associated with a greater likelihood of being married, and to being married to spouses with greater incomes.[18] Skin color, in romance as well as in many other contexts, bespeaks power.

Even the feet can be a source of romantic attraction. In long-ago China, bound feet were a measure of beauty as well as of social status, with the latter being secured by an advantageous marriage. Where the custom was popular, footbinding was essential to landing a husband. Especially for women of the lower classes, footbinding afforded the opportunity to "move upward in the marriage and service market." For women in the upper classes, footbinding served as a symbol of their existing status.[19] During the antifootbinding movement, women with bound feet, often prostitutes, concubines, or wives of conservative families, were displayed with the bindings removed. The women were humiliated into removing their bindings and experienced extreme pain when trying to walk without the bindings. But the heaviest punishment they experienced with their unbound feet was the loss of economic and social status.[20] Keep this in mind for a later discussion of foot beautification surgery for romantic and economic reasons (in Chapter 6).

The Effect of Children's Looks

Romance, as it happens, sometimes results in children. And appearance issues persist in the nuclear family context such that parents favor attractive children over unattractive children. Mothers of less-than-attractive newborns do not spend as much time holding the baby close, staring into the baby's eyes, or talking to the baby as they do with attractive newborns; instead, their attention is much more easily deflected from the less attractive babies.[21] In a new study (2005), it is reported that parents treat their children differently, as observed in supermarkets, depending on how attractive the children are. In short, parents are more protective of and attentive to attractive children, making sure, for example, that the attractive children were safely strapped into the grocery cart. Meanwhile, parents let their unattractive children out of their sight and allowed them to wander more than 10 feet away without apparent notice or concern.[22]

Abused children under court protection are disproportionately unattractive, with abusive parents possibly reacting to the children's unattractiveness as signals of poor health or viability. In support, other studies show that mothers favor the healthier of twins, with the explanation being that parents have, historically, faced limited and uncertain resources, and less healthy-looking (less attractive) babies may have been viewed as less likely to survive and thus riskier investments.[23]

Sexism abounds in parental views on their children's size, with mothers having double standards for their heavy sons and heavy daughters.[24] Mothers are more likely to identify daughters as "overweight" than sons of the same size. Of children who are at-risk of being overweight but not yet overweight, mothers reported their daughters as overweight three times as often as they did their similar-weight sons. Not to blame mothers too much, since we might assume that women, being the major victims of looks-bias, are understandably more sensitive to appearance issues, but consider an example of mother-daughter bonding over footbinding. In Wang Ping's analysis of footbinding, she writes: "Through pain and mutilation [altered women's bodies] became the codes of beauty, femininity, and eroticism."[25] Ping also describes repeatedly the female bonding that comes about from footbinding, such as when mothers bind their daughters' feet, sharing the pain and later the power and glory of tiny feet. Reading this passage in Ping's book prompted me to wonder about the effects of heavy women bonding with each other and with their daughters over concerns about weight, all sharing the bad experiences they have faced because of their size. Women who are not even overweight but worry about being overweight, as well as overweight women who hate their size and are familiar with the anxiety and self-loathing that comes about from social attitudes toward obesity, may feel very strongly about their daughters' size. They may glory in their daughters' thinness, as generations-ago Chinese mothers did in their daughters' tiny feet, and fret over their own and their daughters' weight gain.

Media Influence on How We View Sex and Looks

Of course, the media play a significant role in associating good looks and sexual desirability. Beer ads subtly inform us that if we drink the beer advertised, we will have a great deal of luck attracting beautiful people. In an amusing turn, the Advertising Standards Authority in Britain is hoping to curb binge drinking by substituting "overweight, middle-aged, [and] balding" male models in drink ads. Until lately, Lambrini, a popular party drink, featured very attractive women (the "Lambrini Girls") chasing after attractive "hunky" young men and, naturally, catching them. The ad regulators worried that the association between sex with beautiful people and drinking would encourage irresponsible drinking. Hence, an unattractive man replaced the hunk: if the man in the ad is unattractive, it negates the message that drinking brings sexual-social success.[26]

The melodramedy TV show "Ugly Betty" is about a young woman who is hired in the coveted position of assistant to the chief of a fashion magazine. She is hired because she is "ugly" and thus not a temptation to the not-too-smart chief who previously has had trouble keeping his hands off his more attractive assistants. So far, he is not romantically tempted by the new assistant, presumably because of her looks. Her attractive female coworkers constantly insult and undermine her, out of jealousy and disbelief that "ugly" Betty has landed the job that they feel more qualified for on the basis of looks alone. In reality, Betty is played by an attractive woman, America Ferrera, who has been made up in odd clothes, braces, and thick eyeglasses.[27]

Finally, the media are challenging the way we look at women over age 40. . . sort of.[28] In a news article suggesting that "40 is the new 30," we learn that women are not discounted as unattractive simply because they are not young. But this is contingent upon their being extraordinarily attractive. Women over 40 are acceptable to the viewing public *only if they don't look their age*. In other words, appearance is the key. And, bear in mind that the age-beauty equation is not gender-neutral. Men have generally not been judged harshly when it comes to age. They can be sex objects almost regardless of age: "40 is the new 30" is never even brought up when addressing (media-endorsed) ideals of male beauty. In conclusion, while we are making some moves toward gender-and-looks equalization, we have a long way to go.

CHAPTER 3

Looks and the Workplace

At a meeting of sociologists, the topic of physical appearance and social power was under discussion. The papers presented by the panelists addressed a myriad of topics, such as height, weight, beauty, etc. In the question-and-answer segment, an audience member declared that none of us should be bothered by unfair treatment that we might receive for being less-than-attractive. We should, instead, keep a sense of humor about these slights, as he does. He recounted that his colleagues commonly teased him about his baldness and his paunch, but it doesn't bother him. Without missing a beat, a panelist shot back, "It would if it affected your pay."[1] Our looks do affect our pay. They also affect whether we get jobs in the first place and whether we can retain those jobs. They affect the kinds of jobs we are offered as well as the workplace experience.

It is commonly supposed that "... the good-looking get more money and promotions than average-looking schmoes."[2] A "beauty premium" comes with being tall, slender, and attractive, and is worth roughly an extra 5 percent in pay per hour. There is also, you guessed it, a "plainness penalty," worth about a 9 percent reduction in wages, according to an analysis by the Federal Reserve Bank of St. Louis. It has long been known that taller men are more highly rewarded in business, receiving almost $800 more a year for each extra inch of height. The average CEO is several inches taller than the average U.S. male. It is also well known that heavy people get paid less than thinner people, and this is especially true for women-of-size, with heavy women receiving almost one-fifth less pay than women of "average" weight.[3] All this is not to say that plain and unattractive people are never placed in good jobs. It is particularly true that unionized labor guarantees protections, protections that can be strengthened if violated, against workplace discrimination for any (race, gender, age, and appearance) reason. However, while there are exceptions to the rule, in general, our physical appearance does affect our workplace experience: whether we get jobs and our work experience thereafter.

The kinds of features I mentioned in the introductory chapter are the ones that will get us hired or not: being tall, thin, blonde, clear-skinned, white-toothed, young, and "pretty" or "handsome" does the trick, particularly for some occupations. Broadly, we see a pattern of workplace discrimination against the plain and unattractively featured, against short people, against heavy people, (correlatedly) against racial and ethnic minorities, and against women who either lack the desired Anglo features or are burdened by different rules (aging, in the case of women).

As discussed earlier, we attribute socially desirable traits to attractive people. Attractive people are thought to be more intelligent, easier-to-be-around, more mentally healthy, and more socially skilled than unattractive people. Moreover, and perhaps for these attribution-based reasons, attractive people are favored over equally qualified, less attractive people in decisions to hire, to be recommended for promotion, to be paid higher salaries, and to be positively evaluated as to career potential. "Beauty," as Aristotle put it, "is a greater recommendation than any letter of introduction."[4] The following details workplace bias based on weight, height, plain or unattractive features, age, racial features, disfigurements, and even beauty.

Size and Employment Discrimination

Bias against the overweight is likely, and unfairly, relevant to the bias against less attractive people in general, since, societally, heavy people are not considered attractive.[5] From my readings, there have been a greater number of employment discrimination cases brought by people-of-size than by people deemed unattractive but who are not necessarily heavy. Although it is unknown how many people are discriminated against in the job market because of their looks, size discrimination is probably better documented than discrimination against other physical features, such as beauty, since weight is measurable.

Sometimes size discrimination is not subtle. Mark Roehling talked with heavy people about their hiring experience and cited a case in which a woman was rejected for being, as the interviewer wrote in big letters across the top of her resume, "TOO FAT."[6] Of the over eighty employers Roehling surveyed, many told him flat out that they would not hire a person-of-size: 16 percent considered obesity "an absolute bar to employment" and 44 percent considered obesity as appropriate grounds for passing over an applicant.[7] Roehling also reviewed twenty-nine studies on the extent to which employee weight influences workplace decisions. He found evidence of consistent, significant discrimination against employees-of-size at virtually every stage of the employment cycle, including selection, placement, compensation, promotion, discipline, and discharge. In addition to being evaluated more negatively by management (as subordinates), the overweight are rated less desirable as coworkers (as equals).[8]

The effect of a person's weight on employment experience is greater than the minority traits that we commonly associate with employment discrimination, with the person's weight influencing workplace discrimination more than gender, race and ethnicity, and disabilities. (This is probably the case because, mostly, there are no laws against size discrimination as there are against other forms of discrimination.) Moreover, coworkers display more negative attitudes toward overweight employees than they do toward ex-felons or ex-mental patients.[9]

The National Association for the Advancement of Fat Acceptance surveyed its membership regarding employment discrimination. Of the 1,200 questionnaires, it was found that 62 percent of very heavy women, 31 percent of moderately heavy women, and 42 percent of heavy men were not hired for a job because of their weight. The most common comment made by survey respondents was that they suspected weight discrimination but could not prove it. This means that the reported percentage of job discrimination cases may actually be an underestimate of the true incidence.[10]

Historically, workplace discrimination based on physical appearance was founded on health issues, in combination with aesthetics issues. Such discrimination started around 1900 but heightened after WWII when employers began to "systematically exclude overweight applicants on the grounds that their girth would interfere physically or aesthetically with their job performance, a trend that notched up still further by the 1970s as businesses sought to combat health costs by excluding poor insurance risks."[11] Strictly aesthetically speaking, female service workers (such as flight attendants) became a principal target of size discrimination, noticeably in the 1970s. Discrimination leveled at them is assuredly and principally appearance-based.

We know that the issue of size and the workplace is as much if not more about aesthetics than it is about health care costs because, comparing smoking and weight as factors in employment, the overweight are treated with more discrimination by employers than smokers. For example, in the 1980s the U-Haul rental company charged overweight employees an extra insurance premium but did not overcharge smokers.[12] Smoking (until the early 1990s), cancer-causing tanning, driving over the speed limits, and other destructive activities are viewed as less health-hazardous than being overweight. Part of the explanation for weight discrimination, especially as compared to employees' hazardous activities and poor states of health, is the self-control issue that keeps cropping up in any discussion of body size. "Alcoholics might be sick... fat people should be able to control themselves."[13]

What Does Size Have To Do with It Anyway?

The immediate question is: what does size have to do with the ability to do a job? This question has been raised and answered in many fora, and will be discussed in more detail in the chapter on looks and the legal community (Chapter 8). To cut to the chase, size, or any parameter of looks has little or nothing to do with the capacity for work. Yet we see that entertainers, flight attendants, personal trainers, cosmetic counter workers, and others are judged by inappropriate-to-the-task standards of physical appearance. Let us consider the case of Deborah Voigt, the renowned opera soprano. Ms. Voigt was dropped from a production of Strauss's "Ariadne auf Naxos" by the Royal Opera House at Covent Garden because of her size, not because of any quality about her voice, and was replaced by a slimmer soprano. The role, in this version of the opera, called for Ms. Voigt to wear a little black cocktail dress. Her voice was as sensational as always; it was her size that lost her the job. She recognized immediately that a social attitude toward people-of-size is "the last bastion of open discrimination in our society," yet she wanted to keep working.[14] She has since undergone gastric bypass surgery, a dangerous weight-loss procedure, resulting in a loss of 100 pounds.[15]

Size and Compensation

A lot of the size-work discrimination issue centers around health, such that people-of-size are thought to be a liability because of presumed weight-related medical problems and lost productivity. According to a 2002 study by the Rand Corporation, obesity is a greater cause of chronic illness than smoking, alcoholism, and poverty. Thus, the reasoning goes, health care costs are higher for the overweight than for any other group studied, except the elderly. So, on the assumption that they will be sick more often, people-of-size are paid less since it is presumed that they will use more of the employer-funded health insurance and they are forced to pay more for health insurance.[16]

In another study, using Bureau of Labor Statistics data, Stanford University researchers found that employers may be compensating for the expected higher health costs of workers-of-size by giving them slimmer paychecks. But here's the tricky part: it is not clearly determined that obese employees' health costs are actually higher. While it has long been documented that severely overweight workers get paid less than other employees, there is no clear indication that overweight workers should legitimately be considered riskier on health parameters. The Stanford study found that the pay gap exists in workplaces with employer-paid health insurance, suggesting that the lower wages are in compensation for the *expected* greater medical expenses of people-of-size. It has been shown that yearly medical expenses are higher on average ($732 per year higher) for the overweight than for the nonoverweight but it has also become known that the wage penalties *exceed* these health care costs, making the discrepancy look very much like punishment for one's size. The situation is not one of cost sharing by all, with the lighter-weight workers sharing the medical costs of obesity-related conditions such as diabetes and hypertension. Rather, the research shows that workers-of-size are paying these costs themselves by collecting smaller paychecks. The overweight, according to this study are being paid almost $5,000 a year less than their thinner coworkers, and that the "magnitude of the wage penalty exceeded the expected marginal cost of insuring an obese worker." In sum, there isn't any solid, inarguable reason for this wage penalty.[17]

Heavy men experience wage penalties, but only when they exceed the highest weight levels.[18] Heavy women fare worse: on average, overweight women earn nearly $7,000 less a year than their thin counterparts, with greatly overweight women earning 24 percent less.[19] Women-of-size don't have to weigh very much for employment discrimination to kick in.[20] Bafflingly, women can be discriminated against for being too fat even when they are thin. "Even thin people, especially women, can be perceived as being too fat. Once regarded this way, they may find themselves suddenly substantially limited in the major life activity of working. Scores of slender flight attendants have found themselves in this situation."[21]

Size as Disability

One route that people-of-size can pursue in workplace discrimination is to claim discrimination against a disability instead of discrimination against their weight per se. This practice actually works pretty well, or at least better than claiming weight discrimination. But it is not a route that a lot of heavy people want to take, for good reason. People-of-size commonly argue that they are not disabled, and that they are perfectly capable of doing the same job as thinner workers.[22]

In order to invoke the Americans with Disabilities Act of 1990 or the Rehabilitation Act of 1973, the plaintiff must establish that she or he has a disability but is otherwise qualified for the job in question. The plaintiff must substantiate that her or his capacities are limited enough as to require protection under the law, but "not so limited as to be rendered unable to perform the essential functions of the job with reasonable accommodations. This has not been an easy task for overweight individuals. . . ."[23] To establish a disability because of obesity, the employee must be able to prove that he or she is 100 percent over ideal weight ("morbidly obese") or that her or his size is a symptom of a physiological condition. Mostly, these conditions do not apply and therefore are not helpful to the vast majority of people-of-size who are not 100 percent over the "ideal" weight or whose size is a result of a medical condition. Plus, as mentioned, weight-based discrimination extends to the mildly obese, and to women who are not even obese, but merely above ideal weight.[24]

Returning to the point that many people-of-size are opposed to seeing themselves as disabled, to define large body mass as a disability flies in the face of the struggle "to be accepted and regarded as 'normal.'" The fat-acceptance community views this fat-approximates-disability as "an effort to further stigmatize them. They feel that it is not their bodies that cause problems, but society's treatment of them as unable, different, undeserving, and inferior."[25] The real issue is one of societal bias rather than inability to do the job.[26]

For that matter, the disabled are not, on the whole, fond of the idea of people-of-size being included in the disabled category. A portion of the disabled community are instead downright hostile about including heavy people, with some disabled-rights advocates expressing the view that including overweight people, a group that engenders such widespread disrespect, would set back their movement. One of the sticking points of resistance by the disabled-rights community is the fat-by-choice assumption. Not only are the overweight the subject of widespread and vehement derision, an equally strong social attitude is that size is mutable-at-will.

While there is little dispute that disability is not under one's control, the common social view shared by the mainstream public and the disability-rights community is that fat is voluntary.[27]

So declaring size as a disability is not an effective or even relevant route for most heavy people seeking remedies against workplace discrimination. Some in the fat-acceptance community, medical profession, and legal profession argue that "only the super-sized [morbidly obese in medical terms] should be included under the category 'disabled,' noting that they often have different health concerns, different access problems, and suffer greater social stigma."[28] In sum, people-of-size are vulnerable to workplace discrimination and are without solid legal protection. Protection against weight-based discrimination, where it does exist, falls to state and local statutes. Santa Cruz, San Francisco, Washington DC, and the state of Michigan are the only places (at this writing) with laws prohibiting weight-based discrimination.[29]

Discrimination by Height, Beauty, Youth, and Race

And then there is the other dimension of size, height, as a barrier to employment. Though superbly trained, lawyer Paul Steven Miller had a very rough time getting a job. His sparkling resume attracted the attention of tens of prestigious law firms; yet, once the employers met him in interviews, he was rejected. By way of "explanation," he is 4 feet and 5 inches tall. This difference, a senior partner explained, "might scare away clients." He did land a job as a professor at the University of Washington, where he is much admired by his students, and has been successful, very successful, in equal-employment law. One of his achievements is the development of the national-level Alternative Dispute Resolution Program, which aims to resolve workplace discrimination claims before they go to court.[30]

Of course, height is about image rather than ability. Corporations prefer to hire men with above-average height, with more than half of the CEOs in American Fortune 500 companies being 6 feet or taller, supposedly because these men fit an "image." Short men and any-height women can do the job as well as tall men but they do not, according to the people doing the hiring, fit the image. Once hired, height significantly impacts salaries, and this is true across a wide range of jobs and across genders: height has substantial effects on pay for both genders, with the effects being greater for men. In the case of height, the "advantage to the tall would not be discriminatory if tall people outperformed the short on the job. But these studies are of office workers and executives, not basketball players, and there were no differences in the quality and quantity of work performed, based on height."[31]

One would think that at least in Communist China looks would not be a barrier to employment and that equal treatment would be more dependent upon ability than looks. But even here we find denial of jobs based on looks, not meritocracy. A woman was denied a job as a legal affairs officer on the grounds that she is half an inch too short (5 feet 1 inch). She is only one of many Chinese denied government jobs because they do not meet government qualifications for height, looks, and "robust health," an often unwritten hiring code of physical appearance. The rejected woman said that the government is "trying to attract the tallest or the prettiest people" because such standards make the government (and Chinese society as a whole) look good. These looks-based labor practices point to sexism. In Hunan Province, for instance, women seeking government jobs had to demonstrate that they had symmetrically shaped breasts. Luckily, after women expressed their outrage publicly, the requirement was dropped. One successful challenge does not a pattern make, however. Candidates for flight attendant jobs with the government-run Nanchang Institute of Aeronautical Technology are (currently, as of my last reading) asked to parade on stage in swimwear. In another example, besides showing general aptitude and proficiency in English, a "bikini test" is required as part of a comprehensive examination with the school system. Especially for internationally visible jobs, China applies rigorous requirements for height, physique, and beauty. The underlying explanation as to how employers can get away with these requirements is not unlike what can be said of the United States and other countries with surpluses of labor: "The government has the choice of so many millions of people, so officials think they can be as picky as they want."[32]

Abercrombie and Fitch aggressively seeks young, white, good-looking sales staff, excluding others who do not possess these characteristics. Hispanic, African American, and Asian job-seekers who have been denied employment on the sales floor (the better-paying jobs) were steered by Abercrombie and Fitch store managers toward the stockroom. According to an Abercrombie and Fitch employee, attractive white people could admit to no retailing experience but would be hired because they fit the image, while those with a lot of retail experience but without pretty faces are passed over. Abercrombie and Fitch officials proudly acknowledge that they purposely build a pretty and handsome sales force, and industry experts say this is a steadily growing trend in American retailing. Businesses, including the cosmetics giant L'Oreal, the Gap, and the W hotel chain openly seek workers who are sexy, sleek, and good-looking. The Benetton clothiers pride themselves on hiring good-looking people from a variety of ethnic groups, instead of going the Abercrombie and Fitch route of hiring "classic American" (blue-eyed, blonde) looks to represent them in stores, on the Web site, and as models for their catalogs.[33]

Age has a significant overlap with perceived beauty. Physical beauty, as society interprets it, peaks young. Extreme beauty is rare in any case, but when it does occur, it occurs in the young (usually considered less than age 35).[34] And, of course, there is the aggravating factor of gender. Hollywood leading men can be almost any age, but this is not so for women.[35] I recall Robert Redford saying recently that he would not consider getting a facelift. He doesn't need one, not because he's not getting craggy-looking, but because it doesn't matter if he does get craggy-looking. For now, let's consider the case of a cosmetics counter worker, fired for not being young and "hot enough."

A regional sales manager of L'Oreal was ordered by a top executive to fire a saleswoman in the perfume department for "not being sexy enough." She was further told, "Get me somebody hot." The sales manager was given no legitimate reason to fire the "capable, perfectly presentable employee" and refused to do it. So the sales manager was let go also. She sued, successfully, on the grounds that the state's (California's) fair employment law, which bars sexual discrimination, had been violated. The wording in the case is interesting in its recognition of the subjectivity of beauty as well as sexism: "An explicit order to fire a female employee for failing to meet a male executive's personal standards for sexual desirability is sex discrimination."[36] In a similar gender- and looks-biased instance, federal courts have found it illegal for airlines to apply different weight restrictions for female and male flight attendants. Until these legal findings, female flight attendants were subject to far more severe weight limits than men doing the same job. However, there remains plenty of room for looks-gender discrimination. Employers can legally "take attractiveness into account for female employees when it is a *bona fide qualification*, as with fashion models or movie stars."[37] In the conclusion, we will return to this notion of bona fide qualifications.

Naomi Wolf's instructive book on the beauty myth tells us that, "The job market refined the beauty myth as a way to legitimize employment discrimination against women."[38] Women have been taught that we must be as beautiful as we can be, that beauty is a major source of capital, and that being beautiful, if not ensuring success, will help propel us forward more than not being beautiful. Yet, as Wolf clearly points out, these teachings are not really true. With the women's movement, women demanded, and gained, some access to power. But our advancement was stunted when rules changed (we now have to be more beautiful than ever before) and when double standards are applied (as when being *too feminine* and *too pretty* can sabotage our best efforts).[39] "Beauty discrimination," Wolf writes, "has become necessary, not from the perception that women will not be good enough, but that they will be, as they have been, twice as good."[40] Nonachievable and ever-shifting standards such as these pose a worrisome new twist to workplace bias.

The main characteristic I have been describing here is beauty, but beauty (as socially defined) is not entirely disparate from race, ethnicity, gender, age, and disability. A question raised about such discriminant hiring, to which I will return at the end of this chapter, is: If a corporation's success and failure are dependent upon hiring good-looking people and excluding unattractive or plain people, couldn't such a practice be excused as just market forces at work, in the same way that the more qualified (even if based on appearance) person *should* legitimately get the job? Well, no. Though not necessarily illegal, selecting only people with the "right" looks (young, white, etc.) becomes contentious when racial and other forms of discrimination are clearly occurring, whether this discrimination is intentional or otherwise. The Equal Employment Opportunity Commission (EEOC) has accused several companies of race and age discrimination by favoring good-looking, young, white people in hiring. Yet this pattern of hiring by beauty continues and is especially prevalent at upscale businesses and is increasing.[41] Perhaps the lean economic times encourage employers to be as picky as they want, giving them wide range to apply suspect criteria, such as physical appearance, to their employment decisions.

"Unattractiveness," Disfigurements, and the Workplace

Samantha Robichaud has a dark purple "port wine" stain on her face, which has prevented her from getting a management position at McDonald's fast food restaurant. She had an excellent work record at her McDonald's grill job, where she was not in the public eye but, though perfectly qualified, she has been refused promotion to a managerial position. After many tries, finally, she was told the real reason for denial. Her disfigurement, she was told, would scare off customers and make babies cry. After contacting the EEOC, the conclusion was reached that she had been improperly discriminated against. The acting director of the Americans with Disabilities Act (ADA), which also became involved in the case, said, "This is no different from a whole line of cases in which employers said, 'We can't hire someone who's black for this kind of position because our customers would be uncomfortable.' That's illegal discrimination, and it's no different here." Ms. Robichaud is not disabled, but McDonald's is viewing her so and thus disqualified her for a manager's position. Though not disabled, the employment discrimination she is facing is due to a physical difference beyond her control.[42]

Virginia Postrel seems to disagree that Ms. Robichaud should be treated fairly. She recounts the EEOC case accurately, that Ms. Robichaud was denied a visible (front counter managerial) job because of her looks, and that she had worked at other McDonald's jobs admirably. Postrel, however, denies the validity of the EEOC ruling that: "The opportunity to make a living and succeed in the workplace is not restricted to models and movie stars but is the promise held out to every person with talent, skills, and ambition." Instead, Postrel argues, "The EEOC is using a sympathetic client to outlaw a perfectly natural, if unkind, phenomenon: preferring good-looking employees to unattractive ones." Here, one might question in what way this phenomenon of looks-based bias is "perfectly natural." The EEOC, Postrel goes on to say, is "effectively trying to define ugliness as a disease." A more obvious interpretation of the EEOC ruling is that it is an attempt to outlaw discrimination based on physical features over which we have no control.[43]

It could be worse. Ms. Robichaud could be fat. Given the discrimination that the disfigured encounter in employment and other arenas of social life, it may be less than that faced by people-of-size. As shown by a recent survey, 38 percent of craniofacially disfigured adults (those with disfigurements to the front of the face and head) experience discrimination in employment *or* social settings. Amazingly, though 38 percent is a very large portion of people facing stigmatization, especially for something beyond their control, this figure is substantially less than the rates of discrimination women-of-size reported in hiring decisions alone.[44]

When Beauty Backfires

Attractive men have a greater chance of being hired, at better pay, and of being promoted than unattractive men. The relationship between attractiveness and employment success is less straightforward for women.[45] On the whole, attractive women, as with attractive men, stand a better chance of getting hired and receiving higher salaries. Some studies show, however, that feminine beauty can backfire. For example, attractive women have been found to be less likely to be made partners in law firms. And beauty can work to a woman's disadvantage in seeking a managerial job, requiring snap decisions and the capacity to withstand pressure. The problem seems to be that beauty is falsely equated with submissiveness, bringing on unwarranted assumptions that attractive women are "submissive and overly sexual rather than tough and decisive," and hence not management material. Beauty works to a woman's advantage if she is seeking a clerical job with high visibility and low pay, though.[46]

There is no basis to the assumption that a pretty woman is less capable than a plain one or an attractive or plain man. Mostly, as with race, gender, age, etc., our looks are not a matter of choice and, just as importantly, have nothing to do with our abilities to be good workers, friends, students, romantic partners, and so on. But just for the sake of understanding, consider Thorstein Veblen's analysis of nonworking women as status objects for rich men. In 1899, Veblen wrote his *Theory of the Leisure Class*, in which he complained of women wearing high-heeled shoes and corsets. These devices, he argued, prohibited women from working, which suited their wealthy men (who didn't need a second income from their spouses) who could then better control their nonworking wives. Thus women, at least those married to economically stable men, became status objects via these beautifying devices rather than viable workers.[47] Perhaps this is the source of our prejudice against women of beauty: that they are made incapable by their beautifying devices. Or perhaps we simply assume, wrongly, that beautiful women have not had to work as hard to get ahead. If there is any truth to this assumption, it is not a wholesale truth since plenty of attractive women do work very hard. At any rate, the "boopsey" effect exists. If "women are too gorgeous, people assume they are airheads."[48]

To add insult to injury, attractive women are more likely to be the victims of sexual harassment by male coworkers.[49] Wolf reports the case of a "young and 'beautiful' and carefully dressed" woman who was subject to sexual harassment, fondling, and rape by her employer. In a resulting court case, the court decided against her, ruling that her appearance and her manner of dress was provocative and that she invited the abuse. In another case, in which a woman did not want to be provocative in the slightest, she lost her job because she would not "walk more femininely, talk more femininely, dress more femininely," or "wear make-up."[50] Women, it seems, can be too sexy, too pretty, or too dressed-to-please. Or they can be too none of these things. Either way, if women are too pretty or not pretty enough, they can find themselves in a double bind.

In the next, concluding section, double standards will figure large. But before leaving this topic, let me interject that handsome men, while it may not affect their being hired or the salaries they earn, are also sometimes objectified. To quote Paul Newman: "To work hard, as I've worked, to accomplish anything, and then have some yo-yo come up and say, 'Take off those dark glasses and let's have a look at those blue eyes' is really discouraging."[51] To be judged on one's looks, no matter the gender and no matter what those looks are, is regressive, economically and otherwise, for society and its individual members.

(Ir-)Rational Bias

Finally, let us look at some rationales for workplace discrimination. First, there is the "rational bias theory," which explains that external pressure from superiors or from clients can justify discrimination. In such cases, even though the employment decision-maker may lean toward equal treatment, they feel pressure to discriminate against, say, the overweight or the unattractive. We saw this justification in the Robichaud case in which McDonald's said that having Ms. Robichaud in the public eye would frighten the customers. Justifying discrimination in this manner, we find hiring decisions being influenced by predicted negative reactions of customers and coworkers; thus, hiring decisions are based on fear of alienating others outweighing equal treatment.[52]

Then there is "valid discrimination." This form of discrimination rationale defers to the possibility that "some stereotypes have a basis in fact, and that in some circumstances, reliance on stereotypes can promote predictive accuracy."[53] For instance, there is some debatable-but-presented-as-factual support for the relationship between obesity and health problems. So long as there is any indication that this relationship has validity, that heavy people are more likely to be absent from work or to have health problems prohibiting their work capacity (in other words, that the stereotypical inferences about overweight employees are true), discrimination against them is "valid."[54]

And lastly, there is the "professional beauty qualification" or PBQ. As Naomi Wolf tells it, "before women entered the work force in large numbers, there was a clearly defined class" of women whose work it was to be beautiful. They were in the "display professions" as actors, dancers, and sex workers; they were of low and disrespected status. Compared to previously, women in the display professions today earn more money and possess more status. The problem is, ordinary women who want to enhance their employment (or other social) status are expected to emulate these display women. Now, "all the professions into which women are making strides are being rapidly reclassified . . . as display professions." That which the U.S.

sex discrimination laws refer to as a bona fide occupational qualification (BFOQ) is now the PBQ. In short, with attractiveness being a "require-ment" for many jobs, the PBQ has become "a parody of the BFOQ."[55] The PBQ is defended as being "nondiscriminatory with the disclaimer that it is a necessary requirement if the job is to be properly done."[56] Not unexpectedly, the ever-expanding PBQ is applied overwhelmingly as an employment standard for women rather than men since the *real* purpose of the workplace PBQ is gender discrimination. Legal arguments aside, if looks are a bona fide part of the job, and a woman doesn't meet or exceed those appearance standards, she can, litigation-free, be fired or not hired in the first place. As women became economic forces to be reckoned with, the sexist economic structure needed a response, a counterapproach, to keep us in our places, and the PBQ filled the bill. It has been traditionally the case that we had to be attractive to improve our stations in life (work, romance, and other) but now the ante is upped. Beauty has become merely the starting point, the necessary if not sufficient "condition for a woman to take the next step" to improve her life chances in her work or in other roles.[57]

I started out, in the introductory chapter, discussing subjectivity. Looks standards are subjective enough that legal questions on the topic of phys-ical appearance are left unresolved or unsatisfactorily resolved. As Wolf summarizes, "A woman can be fired for not looking right, but looking right remains open to interpretation." Indeed, in 1979, a federal court de-termined that employers have the right to set appearance standards.[58] To the extent that beauty is not objective, a society's power structure can agree to raise beauty standards, and we are expected to reach or surpass these standards if we are to be socially successful.[59]

Women in the workplace teeter over a precarious double-standard precipice. They are expected to be feminine and businesslike simulta-neously, according to sociologist Deborah L. Sheppard. This is a difficult task, to serve simultaneously two possibly contradictory roles, especially given the shifting and arbitrary standards. And this dilemma is restricted to women; men, for the most part, do not experience the same contradiction.[60]

PART 2

The Pressures

CHAPTER 4

The Diet, Fitness, and Supplements Industries

Most of us are dissatisfied with our looks, and we are so because the world outside ourselves tells us we should be. Since this is the case, many of us participate in the diet, fitness, and supplements industries. We buy the diet books and eat the expensive prepared diet food. We adhere at least momentarily to exercise programs, buy the gym equipment, gym memberships, and workout videos. We ingest diet pills, vitamins, supplements, steroids, and hormones that promise weight loss, muscle gain, or height enhancement knowing that these substances may be harmful. The pressure is enormous to change our bodily appearance. These alterations or hoped-for alterations are undertaken in order to improve our chances in work, romance, and other avenues to social power as described in the first part of the book.

Before we get into the heart of the matter, let me explain briefly why I'm using the word "industry." The amount of money that the public pours into these avenues for changing our appearance is staggering, but so is the capital invested by the corporations that convince us to buy their products and services. For example, in 2003, weight-control products and services, including drugs, diet and exercise programs as well as bariatric surgery, amounted to $15.2 billion.[1] Given this public-corporate exchange of capital, as I will describe here and in the next two chapters on cosmetics and plastic surgery, we definitely have a sense of a beauty "industry."

Diet Industries and the Pressure to be Thin

In my mail, I receive as perhaps do many people, advertisements for weight loss. Two brochures about weight-loss drugs promise to make your friends envious. "My friends think I had plastic surgery. They're very jealous!" exclaims an attractive young woman (pictured) in a testimonial. She says that she has reduced her size to a "sexy size 6."[2] In this brochure, entitled *Plastic Surgery Magazine* (which, as near as I could tell, did not advertise or offer plastic surgery), there are a number of other pictures of attractive, white people, some of them posed as happy couples. The selling point is "a new pill [which] may work better than liposuction," as advertised by a physician or a man posing as a physician. We are further told that we needn't give up eating fats: "Fat-free is not the answer." With new "zymax," we can increase our "thermogenesis up to 600 percent in just minutes." Having thoroughly read the brochure, I remain very much in the dark as to what thermogenesis is.

Another brochure sitting on my desk is called *Prevention* and it promises that, through the use of "the right combination of nature's magic," we can flatten our tummies fast, solve our cellulite problems, "look 10 pounds thinner" (note: not *be* 10 pounds thinner), reshape our bodies in record time (3 weeks), and be happy. We can have all this and it requires "no extra effort" on our parts. Indeed, we can "eat gooey, yummy foods and lose weight." To illustrate, a young, attractive, thin woman is shown eating chocolate cake with whipped cream. The brochure offers to sell us a booklet (a reference guide) with a combination of vitamins, herbs, minerals, supplements, fruits, vegetables, teas, and grains that will do the trick, to make us "happy, slim, and sexy."[3]

All-you-can-eat diet proponents claim scientific evidence that it's the *kind* of food you eat rather than the *amount* that makes a difference. So "you can eat more frequently, eat a greater quantity of food, and still lose weight and keep it off!... And forget about exercising too. If one only mixed the right foods, why, 'you can burn more fat watching TV than by exercising.'"[4]

Fat became a four-letter word after WWII, when the "diet and fitness industries burgeoned and fostered a mass obsession with weight and body shape."[5] Unfortunately, no matter how devotedly we succumb to the pressure to be thin, most diets have not worked as promised. We have all heard stories about the wide variety of diets (South Beach, Atkins, Scarsdale, etc.), and perhaps the reader has experienced these endless variations on diets themselves, all promising to be the one that will work.[6] Studies from the National Institutes of Health show that if people lose weight by dieting, they regain it within 5 years, with two-thirds of them regaining within 1 year. Other studies show that diets fail nearly all (95 percent to 98 percent) of the time. [7] These findings immediately raise the question of why diets fail, since it makes perfect sense that if one takes in fewer calories and only the right kind of calories, one would lose weight and keep it off. Some writers on the topic of failed diets, for example, Greg Critser and Jean Renfro Anspaugh, say that the "failed" dieters cheat. Others say that even those who strictly adhere to their diets are genetically sabotaged by their inherent physical anatomies, which operates as an hydraulic system: when the calories get too few, the body uses them more efficiently so that the dieter cannot maintain weight loss. [8]

Because diets don't work as advertised, we can address the diet industry in terms of its capitalist motivations. A capitalist economy relies on consumers consuming, being dissatisfied with the results of their consuming, and thus consuming more. Hillel Schwartz writes, "The diet is the supreme form for manipulating desire precisely because it is so frustrating." [9]

Peter Stearns, writing of diet books and diet foods, finds that in the post-WWII United States, the diet industry took off like a rocket. Diet books multiplied and monopolized the bestseller list. Moreover, between 1950 and 1955, diet soft drink sales soared 3,000-fold. Metracal and other food substitute products were introduced very successfully as were national weight-reducing chains. [10] Women were the primary targets of these marketing strategies, with most diet books and the majority of commercial programs having been directed toward women. [11] In substantiation, we find that 90 percent of the diet pill prescriptions are made out to women. [12]

Writing of weight-loss industries, Sondra Solovay states: It "is not just the medical establishment that has an interest in keeping fat unacceptable. At $33 to $50 billion per year, the weight-loss industry is a powerful market force completely dependent on convincing people that losing weight is . . . crucial." [13] As a clear indication that diet companies advertise deceptively, she adds that emotional volatility in the ads, such as fear of social rejection, is prevalent. The advertisements, she finds,

take advantage of and perpetuate the fat person's very real experiences with discrimination. Weight-loss advertisements do not condemn employment discrimination against heavy people, they revel in it, proudly producing testimonials from people who got or kept jobs after their weight loss. Nor do they condemn verbal abuse, they use it for their own purposes as they make fat jokes and belittle heavy people. And while the companies may have no moral obligation to do good, these practices actually inflame existing prejudices. [14]

The stereotypes repeated in the advertisements encourage and amplify cultural weight bias. We could, legally, make weight-loss corporations represent their products accurately. A more effective, broader, and longer-lasting approach might be to raise awareness of size-related issues (obesogenic environments and the like) and the consequences of weight bias.

Dieting can be dangerous, particularly when associated with diet pills, and these dangers are not culturally limited. That is, diet pills are not only the purview of the United States, where we have an alleged "obesity epidemic" ongoing. In Singapore, not a country usually associated with an overweight population, there has been a problem with "slim 10" diet pills as used by attractive thin people to stay that way. A beautiful, thin woman grew gravely ill and, as a deathbed plea, begged her family to expose the "growing obsession with being slim." A doctor at a Singaporean eating disorder clinic laments that there is a "rising trend of people falling ill" from eating disorders. Partly, weight fluctuations are the result of affluence and an abundance of food (which is responsible for increasing weight), but also a result of the "barrage of images in the media" (responsible for drastic attempts at weight loss). The Singaporean doctor said that when food was scarce, plump women were sought after; but now that "thin is in," there is "a social expectation" to be very thin.[15]

Let's call the thin-at-all-costs phenomenon the "tyranny of skinny" as does one journalist.[16] Kate Betts writes of fashion's obsession with thinness and bias against fat. And while she acknowledges that there is a growing demand and market for larger-sized clothes (the plus-size market has surged 18 percent in recent years), Gucci and Prada do not make clothes in that size range; indeed, they make nothing larger than a size 12. She superficially mentions liposuction, exercise with personal trainers, and diets as ways to become thinner but her main points are that (a) while some clothing manufacturers, department stores, and runway shows prominently feature plus-size clothes (b) models still are very thin. In 1985, the average fashion model wore a size 8. Today, the average model wears a size 0 or 2.[17] This social demand to be thinner, and thinner still, is curious since the average American is getting bigger, making for a "perverse relationship." But never mind the reality of our growing size: the expectations are that we should be very thin.[18]

We are expected to engage in a "constant vigilance" in our struggle to lose or keep off weight. The Centers for Disease Control and Prevention reported a survey showing that more than two-thirds of Americans (64 percent of men and 78 percent of women) are dieting.[19] These same people also exercise quite a bit in hopes of losing weight or keeping weight from returning. But control is a relative term, according to obesity researchers, meaning that self-control may be no more relevant for the thin as the thick.[20] Some of us are biologically unable to become thin, we can only hope to be less heavy than we are, making self-control seemingly moot in these cases. Only "within certain narrow limits" can we control our weight completely, since we inherit genetic structures that determine our range of body weights, ranges that can vary only about 10 percent from a midpoint, no matter what we do. Chronic dieters, then, through their constant vigilance, are keeping their weight as low as their genes will permit.

We would prefer not to believe that we have so little control over our weight, and the diet industries would be loathe to allow us to believe that we cannot change our appearance. This is an ongoing theme about socioeconomic issues and physical appearance: so long as there is a market for encouraging any kind of looks-altering behavior (dieting *or* overeating), there will be an industry to promote such behavior.

The Pressure to be Big: Steroid Use

Steroids and steroid precursors (legal derivatives of steroids) are used by boys as young as 10 years old "simply because they want to look good." They may also want to bulk up to play sports, but looking good seems to be the growing incentive.[21] In U.S. high schools and off-campus gyms, students, particularly nonathletic students, use bodybuilding drugs to achieve an athletic body image. Almost half a million U.S. teenagers use steroids, and steroid use by high school seniors has increased nearly 50 percent while use of other illegal drugs has stabilized or dropped.[22]

The risks of steroid use apparently do not matter to those who ingest them. Admittedly, the risks of steroid use are unclear.[23] To make matters more confusing, society sends mixed messages about steroid use: on the one hand, we should strive to be strong and muscular; yet, on the other hand, we should not take steroids because they're dangerous and a form of cheating when used by athletes. Historians of looks-and-society have pointed out that, as muscles became more desirable for ordinary men and women, steroid use became prominent in sports and bodybuilding. In other words, cultural changes such as a reverence for muscles made steroid use more appealing. Witness dolls as role models. A comparison of G. I. Joe dolls from 1982, 1992, and the mid-1990s illustrates "how widespread the desire for muscular bodies has become."[24] The change in the dolls' physiques is amazing, from a normal-looking representative of the human race to something that truly is not realistic. The same can be said of Barbie, who has gone through a number of physical iterations, though none of them realistic. Barbie is not a representative steroid queen, of course. She does not ripple with muscles but is instead incredibly and unrealistically thin.

And, sure enough, boys are not the only ones using steroids. A growing and worrisome number of U.S. girls, some as young as 9 years old, are using bodybuilding steroids. And they are ingesting these drugs for the same reason as the young boys— "to get the toned, sculpted look of models and movie stars"—not necessarily to get an athletic edge in sports. Not uncommonly, these steroid-using girls also abuse diuretics, amphetamines, and laxatives to lose weight and, on the whole, have eating disorders. Because drug use and anorexia are secretive behaviors, it is unknown just how many young girls engage in these severe measures to lose weight, but it has been estimated that perhaps 5 percent of high school girls and 7 percent of middle-school girls use anabolic steroids.[25]

The Pressure to be Tall: Growth Hormones

It's good to be tall, socially speaking. Men should be at least 6 feet tall if they want to earn a lot of money, date and marry the most desirable women, win elections, and (in sum) be powerful. We wrongly attribute to taller-than-average men a myriad of positive traits having nothing to do with height: intelligence, talent, competence, trustworthiness, and kindness. Short men, it has been documented, men who are less than the U.S. average of 5 feet and 9½ inches, are more likely to drop out of school, drink heavily, date sparsely, and become emotionally depressed and physically ill. They have less opportunity than tall men of marrying and having children. Their salaries are far less than those of tall men: tall men earn an additional 2 percent annually per inch in height than short men. And we as a public make fun of short men. It is "one of the last acceptable prejudices."[26] Clearly, heightism persists and is an important factor in how we are viewed socially. In a new book, Stephen Hall writes of this "altocracy" as beginning in the first century A.D. with height associated with strength and virtue, to the 1700s with the search for tall (and thus fearsome) soldiers, to today in a society replete with positive stereotypes about tall men.[27]

Really tall women can face some dating and workplace disadvantages, although this prejudice is lessening (see the previous chapter). Petite women (usually considered below 5 feet 4 inches), though they have some social advantages, are less likely to be taken seriously in law, business, and other high-powered professions than are taller women.[28]

We have a solution for the social disadvantages of shortness. The growth hormone, Humatrope, can be administered to perfectly healthy but small children if they are expected to be shorter than 5 feet 3 inches in adulthood. It is an expensive remedy: Growth hormones, as administered to children, cost about $20,000 to $30,000 a year (which may be reimbursed by insurance if the FDA grants approval). Use of such a drug clearly indicates that being short is a "problem," one that can and ought to be fixed. The Eli Lilly pharmaceutical company, which manufactures the growth hormone, refers to shortness as a "growth failure problem," reminiscent of the term "micromastia," which refers to flat-chestedness in women. The term was used by doctors promoting the idea that small breasts are a pathology and that breast implants are the remedy.[29] Similarly, shorter heights is viewed as a deficiency in need of a remedy.

The concern, obviously, is that we will start to view the normal and healthy as a disease. Yes, shortness is a socially disadvantageous trait but it is not unhealthy. A more egalitarian, if not utopian, viewpoint might be that we as a society accept people for what they are (short or tall, heavy or thin, disfigured or not, etc.). However, since we as a society are not totally egalitarian, let us look at the shortness question from where we, as parents and other members of society, are currently. Shortness, though normal, is looked at as a disorder, as something to be treated, when it is compared to the superior trait of tallness. And when we consider that short people do experience reduced life chances, we can, with some imagination, view short people as "disabled." Many parents, wanting to improve their children's future prospects, will administer growth hormones. At the same time, shortness, as a biological-medical phenomenon, is not viewed as an illness equal to other biological-medical phenomena. As Virginia Postrel points out, some biological-medical phenomena "deserve treatment and sympathy and others don't. If you have chronic migraines, we'll help. If you're ugly, too bad." The social assumption, Postrel finds, is that something is very much wrong with being short if we offer a treatment for it. The treatment itself, in other words, proves that (the difference of) shortness is not a good thing. Shortness is a *dislikable* condition, Postrel declares. It is not a painful one (like a migraine) or a life-threatening one (like cancer) or even a condition without sympathy (such as ugliness). It is, rather, a condition that prevents us "from being whom we want to be."[30]

Now, just to turn everything on its head, it has recently been proposed that being short does not have the effect on self-esteem that we thought: Administering Humatrope to short, healthy children to give them a few extra inches in height has no effect on their self-esteem or quality of life. Studies demonstrate that shorter-than-average (for their age group) children are sometimes treated as younger than they are or face some limitations in sports activities, and as a result develop psychological and social problems. And they do possess slightly less ability in social functioning, very likely due to stigmatized treatment. But they exhibit no less self-esteem than their peers.[31] It follows then that the effect of growth hormones, while increasing growth, did not enhance self-esteem, since there was no self-esteem problem in the first place. This leaves us to wonder if the $20,000 to $30,000 paid out for growth hormones is more to satisfy the parents of short children than the children themselves. A physician at a children's hospital insightfully states, "Perhaps efforts toward increasing the height of normal short children should be redirected toward teaching the acceptance of individual differences and placing value on personal character."[32]

As a final illustration of the social impact of height-ism, imagine that law professor Paul Steven Miller (height 4 feet 5 inches), cited in the previous chapter, or sociology professor, Deborah Burris-Kitchen (height 4 feet 9 inches), had, by artificial means, grown tall enough so that they were not of unusual height.[33] The hundreds of students whom they have taught and continue to teach would not be faced with understanding that a person's size is irrelevant to her and his ability, intelligence, likeability, or goodness.

Body Alterations

We modify our bodies in many ways, for many purposes, but mostly to look good, with varying degrees of success. Besides the methods I've mentioned above, we, in various cultures, have bound our feet, elongated our necks, tattooed ourselves, intentionally scarred our faces, and so on. Mostly we do these things in the pursuit of beauty, although we also pursue these alterations to set ourselves apart as a member of a distinct social group (to designate ourselves as "punk," for example) or to signal some change in social status (for instance, the placement of a streak of red vermillion in the parting of the hair on a married Hindu woman).[34] For the most part, in the United States, especially since the 1980s, we engage in these body-altering activities in order to be accepted, to be sought-after romantically or occupationally, to be "buff."[35]

Generally, we shape or attempt to shape our bodies to conform to social ideals of the tall, thin, and muscular. Failing in this endeavor, we disguise our bodies with cosmetic contrivances (molding them into shape) and surgically carve our bodies, as discussed in the next two chapters.

CHAPTER 5

Cosmetics, Cosmeceuticals, and Other Superficial Changes

Cosmetics labels are always careful to state that cosmetics can only aid *in the appearance of* wrinkles, puffy eyes, or other features troubling to the physical appearance. The term cosmetics covers a wide range of products promising a variety of improvements, with the cosmetic industry having made these promises over a long history and continuing to make new promises every day.[1] In 2005, for example, the Dove soap company offered an anticellulite cream that doesn't really remove cellulite (cellulite being the ripply skin texture usually found on women rather than men and usually found on the thighs, the upper arms, and the buttocks). For that matter, no cellulite gel or cream removes cellulite, since cellulite is lumpiness under the skin and the cellulite treatments are topical. The claims made by Dove and other cosmetic manufacturers are based on "pseudoscientific babble" with no "scientific proof that creams make a real, lasting difference." Thus, the advertisers and manufacturers are careful to say that the products reduce the "look of" imperfections.[2]

The Food and Drug Administration defines cosmetics as products that are "rubbed, poured, sprinkled or sprayed on, introduced into or otherwise applied to the human body for cleansing, beautifying, promoting attractiveness or altering the appearance without affecting the body's structure or functions." Since cosmetics do not affect the body's structure or function, obviously, the results of applying them are superficial and temporary. Yet we try them repeatedly, as we have over roughly the past 40,000 years.[3]

While *cosmetics* are the more traditional representation of superficial devices to alter our appearance (such as make-up that conceals flaws or highlights, brightens, and colors the skin), *cosmeceuticals* refer to drugs (pharmaceuticals) as well as treatment products that are less superficial and less temporary than cosmetics. Technically, cosmeceuticals are cosmetic products that are claimed to offer drug-like beauty benefits, at least according to those in the industry.[4]

Cosmeceuticals, a blend of cosmetics and pharmaceuticals, appeared in the 1990s and are most commonly found in the United States although they are increasingly found and used elsewhere as well. Cosmeceuticals are marketed as cosmetics, but contain biologically active ingredients that effect rather than camouflage the user's flaws, such as antiwrinkle creams, baldness treatments, sunscreens, and moisturizers. Cosmeceuticals cause regulatory difficulties for the U.S. FDA and other regulatory agencies, because it is unclear "when a product crosses the line between being merely a cosmetic and becoming a drug, the latter having much more stringent controls on its development, testing, and supply. Much seems to depend on the labeling of the product: one describing itself as a deodorant would probably be classed as a cosmetic, whereas one labeled as an antiperspirant might well be classified as a drug because it claims to close the pores of the skin."[5] Cosmeceuticals can include skincare products like cleansers and moisturizers that contain technologically advanced ingredients, such as antiaging solutions, dermabrasion, glycolic acid peels, and enormously expensive beauty treatment creams (for instance, cle de peau at $475 for an ounce) that according to the ads, make no promises. Yet, chemical peels and microdermabrasion are marketed as making acne scars "a thing of the past."[6] If one is willing to allow a bit more medical intrusion, with the use of lasers, dermatologists can rid us of age spots, and internally ingested drugs are administered in the prevention of acne.

Some cosmeceuticals are available through the drug store and cosmetic counters, and are available for home use without the aid of a technician. Others, such as Botox injections, are available only through, and administered by, a physician or, at the very least, a technician. Dermal fillers, a far more long-lasting procedure than Botox, are administered by dermatologists.[7] As with cosmetics, many of these products are dangerous to use and can cause significant and permanent damage. Also as with cosmetics, some are quite pricey while some are within the buying power of the working class.

In this chapter, I mention a number of contrivances and services intended to alter our appearance superficially and temporarily. Teresa Riordan offers a fascinating history of alterations such as lipstick, mascara, and other make-ups (powder, rouge), but also bust enhancers (inflatable bras, "falsies," and mechanical devices promising to make breasts larger), girdles, bustles, corsets, hair dyes, hair removers (electrolysis, waxing, depilatories), skin treatments (masques, facial massages, and electrons), permanent waves (chemical solutions and rather frightening-looking machines) for hair curling, and nail polish. Her history of beauty treatments describes the significant degree of hucksterism associated with promises not kept, such as little shaver-size rollers alleged to enlarge breasts when rolled over the breasts. Recent cosmetic catalogs advertise a remarkably similar twenty-first-century device, with similar lack of results.

Not surprisingly, "women have been the driving innovative force behind many of these inventions" with, for example, almost two-thirds of "falsies" inventors being women.[8] From Riordan's point of view, these beauty inventions (lipstick, bustles, stiletto heels, etc.) are sources of power for women, with these adornments projecting not only sexuality but also power and status.[9]

The Price of Fleeting Beauty

In the United States alone, cosmetics are a multibillion-dollar industry.[10] Comparing our purchases of reading material to personal care products and services, we, as individuals in the United States, spend more than twice on the latter. Cosmetics, worldwide, are a $45 billion industry, with ineffective thigh creams alone serving a $90 million business.[11]

Cosmeceuticals, by themselves and in contrast to cosmetics, comprise annually a $40 million market.[12] A Botox injection costs about $384, laser hair removal costs $388, microdermabrasion costs $161, collagen injections cost $381, eyelash extension costs $300–500 (with $50–150 for monthly maintenance), and $800 gets you a chemical peel.[13] In short, we spend a great deal of money to look better, even if the results are fleeting or nonexistent.

Social Meaning

All of these superficial changes have social meaning, primarily as indicators of social class. While dentistry isn't new, cosmetic services, such as bonding and whitening for younger-looking smiles, is relatively new and expensive, thus indicating financial strength and leisure time. Eradication of disease, once the purview of the dentistry profession, has been replaced with a new motive: "the enhancement of appearance."[14] Beautiful hands, too, are indicators of idleness. Hands sporting jewels and with long, well-kept nails give the impression of leisure, wealth, and an unacquaintance with work.[15] In times past, types of women's clothing such as metallic cages and layered petticoats (both put under the skirts to make them stand out but also prohibiting free movement), bustles, "trains" (the long trails of skirts), and corsets distinguished those who needn't work from those who must.[16] As always happens, the working- and lower-classes, where possible, imitate the leisurely class; ultimately, these contrivances such as cage crinolines became mass produced, inexpensive, and worn by all classes of women.[17]

Skin Color: A Socially Significant Change

Color of the skin is fraught with meaning because it often refers to social class and ethnicity. Tan skin on white people can refer to leisure time and thus be a false indicator of privilege and higher social status. Whereas, in earlier times, pale skin signified the absence of a need to work outdoors.

Mostly, beauty = light-skinned = employable and socially powerful, with this equation raising the question of why lighter-toned skin is considered more beautiful and why naturally dark-skinned people are pressured to apply skin whiteners. Worldwide, we have witnessed a phenomenal growth in the availability and number of skin-lightening products used in India, Africa, Asia, and the United States (one is called "Fair And Lovely"), the result of a social pairing of fairer complexions with beauty and success. In India, until protested and removed, an ad pictured a young, dark-skinned woman whose father lamented that he had no son to provide for him and his daughter was not earning enough salary. The daughter, it was suggested, could not get a better job or get married unless she lightened her dark skin. She uses the skin lightener, becomes fairer, and (of course) gets a well-paying position as a flight attendant, which "makes her father happy."[18]

In Kenya, we find the same supposition: lighter skin means greater beauty. Here too we find cultural resistance. An African cosmetologist is doing battle against skin lighteners, products that have become "an essential part of many African women's beauty routines and a big business." African social critics state, rightly, that skin lighteners are "merely another negative legacy of white colonialism" and that being white has long been a prerequisite of power and wealth: "The lighter one's skin, it is widely believed here, the wealthier, better educated, and more attractive one is." And, unfortunately, there is plenty of evidence that light skin does indeed lead to greater chances of success. Besides the sheer racism of the pressure to be white, skin-lightening products, which often contain mercury, pose risks of disfigurement (a very unattractive, uneven blotching of the skin) and skin cancer. Yet, apart from the downsides (the racism, disfigurement, and illness), African women remain economically dependent on men, meaning that they need to marry well, due to the same gender-dependent economic disparity that many cultures face. The above-mentioned cosmetologist reminds us, "If the general view is that light-skinned women are more attractive, then it's an investment to try to lighten one's skin. They are not just buying cream. They are buying a dream of a better life."[19]

Race scholars studying skin lightener use in the United States point out that the products are not only race-defining (read: discriminating) and dangerous, but also costly. Skin-bleaching products are a multi-million-dollar industry in the United States, thus we find an "earnings gap between lighter and darker-skinned African Americans."[20]

Under the category of we're-never-happy-with-ourselves, we also find that skin darkening products (self-tanning lotions) and tanning procedures are also in great demand. As with skin lighteners, tans can be very dangerous. But, when health concerns compete with style, "style always wins—in the short term."[21] Tanning is undertaken for aesthetic purposes, although it has some unattractive side effects that reveal themselves later, including wrinkles, saggy skin, age spots, and skin cancer. "Tanorexics" gain the immediate gratification of the admired tan skin, of looking "sexy" and "healthy," neglecting to think of the probabilities of the long-term effects, which usually don't occur for many years.

We never learn, it seems. We have endured serious health problems in our pursuit of beauty. Ancient Greek and Roman women applied toxic lead-based paints to their faces. We have eaten arsenic to make our skin paler in the eighteenth and nineteenth centuries. Tanning, like these other risky behaviors, is driven by vanity and encouraged by images of what we're told we ought to emulate—beautifully tanned models and celebrities.[22]

Body Modifications and Social Status

Tattoos, scarification (intentional and self-administered scarring), piercing, and body paint serve to identify us in terms of gender, age, cultural tastes (music interests, for instance), sexual orientation, and political views. The body is a visible surface that can be decorated to show the individual's interface between herself/himself and society.[23] That is, deliberate scarring, tattoos, and piercing may or may not be viewed as beautifying by their wearers, but beauty is not necessarily the purpose of such decorations. Instead, these alterations serve to set us apart from others; they indicate *social distinctions* or *ranking*.[24] These alterations, which set us apart from the mainstream, can also exclude us from participation in economic and social markets. One illustration would be tattoos, signaling unemployability to some employers.

Body modifying devices like corsets, especially popular during the second half of the nineteenth century, were described by social critic Thorstein Veblen as a *mutilation*, "undergone for the purpose of lowering the subject's vitality and rendering her permanently and obviously unfit for work." As such, the corseted body, at the cost of the wearer's good health, indicated in no uncertain terms that the inhabitant was privileged enough that she needn't work, thus setting her apart from uncorseted women.[25]

Hair Color, Texture, and Removal

Three out of four middle-aged women color their gray hair, as do 13 percent of middle-aged men. But it is not just the middle-aged who color their hair: large numbers of young women color their hair and *larger* numbers of young men are coloring their hair.[26] And it is not just Americans who color their hair: while hair coloring sales in the United States bring in over a billion dollars a year, 60 percent of Japanese and South Korean women color their hair, along with 30 to 40 percent of women in Singapore, Hong Kong, and Taiwan.[27] Probably a goodly proportion of people around the globe color their hair, to look (they believe) more attractive or to disguise their age.

Hair straighteners are not new. Depending on the fashion dictates at any particular time, we may admire or abhor curly hair. Hair texture, clearly, has a racial component to it. African Americans have for decades straightened their hair ostensibly to appear more Caucasian and thus more socially and economically desirable. A change seems to be occurring though, with African Americans straightening their hair less commonly now than in the 1960s. In the 1960s, most African Americans (men and women) straightened their hair. Many, roughly 75 percent of African American women, still use straightening combs and chemical relaxers. Interestingly, it is the upper-middle-class African American women who arrange their hair naturally, in dreadlocks, twists, and Afros. The explanation, not surprisingly, has to do with increased economic power. With increased power, African American women do not need to conform so much to Caucasian standards in the hope of advancing to the middle class.[28]

Bodily hairiness among men comes and goes as a desirable trait, but it is never desirable among women (witness the "bearded lady" of sideshow fame). As with small breasts and short stature, the disease model has been applied to hirsuteness, with excessive hairiness seen as a malady. The American Dermatological Association, in 1877, diagnosed hairiness of the female body with a scary-sounding name: hypertrichosis. And, in 1866, a practitioner of electrolysis (removal of body hair by painful extraction using an electronic tool), referred to the growth of facial hair on women as a deformity.[29] Presently, we use shavers (electric and other), depilatory creams, electrolysis, epilatory machines (small, hand-held devices that pull hair out by the roots), and waxing (which strips the hair by the roots from the skin by means of hot wax and strips of cloth) to rid ourselves of unwanted hair. Yet, we also worry if we don't have enough hair and so we use, with limited success, lotions on our scalps and pharmaceuticals (such as Rogaine) to encourage hair growth. We also wear toupees. We also have hair transplant surgeries, but that is a subject of the next chapter.

The things we do to add or subtract hair are temporary, expensive, and sometimes dangerous. Consider, for instance, eyelash extensions. Eyelash extensions are silk and polyester false lashes, glued to the base of real eyelashes with a very strong adhesive. The procedure must be repeated every 3 to 6 weeks since eyelashes shed. As yet, there are no new regulations pending to deal with the problems that have already come about, such as eyelids being glued to eyeballs, eyelids being glued shut, and bald eyelids.[30]

New Trends: Men and Cosmetics

Men are increasingly using a variety of cosmetics and cosmetic treatments, such as eye gel, premium shave creams, face powder, foundation, brow and eyelash gel, eye shadow, eyeliner, lip gloss, concealer (for blemishes), exfoliating facial scrubs, and other male-specific toiletries. They are doing so for personal and professional reasons. Men, like women, have strong motivations to keep or try to retrieve a youthful appearance; so, as our population ages, it can be assumed, men's use of cosmetics will grow. Euromonitor International, a research group that forecasts market trends, predicts that men's grooming products in the United States alone will grow to almost $4 billion annually.[31] Elsewhere it has been reported that men spend about $95 billion a year on grooming aids and plastic surgery combined.[32]

As the reader can imagine, one hurdle for today's man to overcome is cultural: real men, presumably, don't wear make-up or apply facials.

However, as men age, they are very much aware that they are competing in tight economic markets with younger men and with women. The cosmetic market, not unexpectedly, is willing to accommodate these cultural hurdles by not only supplying men's needs for cosmetic treatments but doing so inconspicuously. In an attempt to be inconspicuous, men may buy their cosmetics at their hairdressers, the dermatologist's office, or over the Internet. And manufacturers of men's cosmetics are careful to call the products "skin care" and "grooming products," not "cosmetics."[33]

Conclusion

Mostly, the reason for the superficial modifications (make-up, etc.) that I have described here is, of course, to beautify. We also want to make a statement about the "special-ness" of our social status; in other words, we want to signify and give meaning to our place in the world. In addition, we undergo procedures to disguise some feature that we would rather the world not know about, for example, our age. Enter Botox and many other temporary and semipermanent remedies. One wonders if we have become a "Botox Nation," as my editor amusingly calls the overfocus on youthful beauty prevalent in the United States and other advanced societies.[34] If so, probably no more than we have been so focused for, say, 40,000 years.

CHAPTER 6

The Plastic Surgery Industry

It seems that the public is fascinated with plastic surgery. Our TV shows reflect this in the popularity of "Nip and Tuck" and "Extreme Makeover." Our entertainment activities are also reflecting a trend toward what we might call recreational surgery. We attend parties at which patients gather in festive arrangements to show off the results of their latest, sometimes multiple, surgeries. "With music throbbing and her proud family looking on," a 16-year-old struts down a runway showing off her brand new nose. Another woman displayed her breast implants. Yet another woman offered her flattened abdomen and wrinkle-free eyelids. Overall, ten women, aged from 16 to 60, proudly displayed their new, slimmer, pumped up or smoothed over body parts at this Long Island "coming out" party where the surgeons showed off their patients "like artists at a gallery opening."[1]

All surgery, including cosmetic, is not without medical danger. The anesthesia alone can pose significant risks. Nor is cosmetic surgery without danger in terms of not meeting the patient's expectations. The unsatisfied are willing to undergo cosmetic surgery, repeatedly, as we find in the "do over." Corrective revision surgeries, or "redos," are often performed because of previous poorly done surgeries, which resulted in uncorrected or worsened features or unanticipated medical complications. Patients may have multiple surgeries on the same site, trying to get the problem (aesthetic or other) corrected. It is not unusual for patients to have undergone as many as a dozen revisions on one body part. Where things get nearly incomprehensible is when the patient has a problem with a revision, then has revision-revision surgery, followed by revision of a revision-revision surgery, and so on. Unfortunately for the patients, the medical risks increase and the likelihood of pleasing cosmetic results decrease with these revisions, mainly because of an accumulation of scar tissue and the loss of cartilage.

Since statistics on redos are not kept or reported, the number of revisions and complications are unknown but are almost certainly underreported. Based on what is known, there has been an increase in such surgery. This increase may be due to a demand for perfect results coupled with a heightened dissatisfaction with one's looks. But another reason for the increase is the fact that more doctors are vying to get into the highly lucrative plastic surgery industry, with plastic surgery being strictly a cash business for the most part, and many of the doctors performing it are not qualified in plastic surgery. Perhaps to the reader's surprise, any medical doctor can perform cosmetic surgery, by virtue of having a license.[2]

Plastic surgery is costly. The charges for plastic surgeries, based on national averages in 2003, are: $5,351 for breast reduction, $3,869 for nose reshaping, $3,360 for breast enlargement, $3,124 for male breast reduction, $3,084 for hair transplants, $2,599 for eyelid surgery, and $2,578 for liposuction.[3]

For all that, in a 10-year period from 1991 to 2001, cosmetic surgeries in the United States have quintupled, with almost 2 million people having had plastic surgery during that time. Our younger generation has fewer qualms about having surgical alterations. Over half (60 percent) of women in the United States and over one-third (35 percent) of men indicate that they would have cosmetic surgery if it were "safe, free, and undetectable."[4]

The Purposes

The history of plastic surgery is lengthy, with most of the modern procedures used dating to the 1880s and 1890s.[5] The purposes of plastic surgery have always been twofold: beautification as well as therapeutic. That is, some surgeries are purely for looks-enhancement, some for health reasons, and some for a combination of the two. Plastic surgery includes a wide range of procedures, such as facelifts to correct the aging of the face, eyelid surgeries to widen Asian eyes and to lift bags, breast implants and breast reduction, liposuction, gastric bypasses, etc. Image-changing surgeries such as rhinoplasty (nose jobs) and rejuvenation surgeries such as facelifts are based on decisions "motivated by both broadly social and narrowly narcissistic impulses, which are in the end interlinked."[6] Other surgeries are more reconstructive or corrective, such as mole removal, nose realignments to aid in breathing, and removal of silicone breast implants to prevent hazardous leakage of the silicone throughout the body.

To make matters more intriguing, the line between reconstructive/constructive and vanity/aesthetic procedures is blurry. *Aesthetic* surgery is, by definition, elective, nonmedical, unnecessary (or not immediately necessary), and for the purpose of vanity. Such procedures are not covered by health insurance, ordinarily, and aesthetic surgery patients "are seen as not really sick."[7] *Reconstructive* surgery, by contrast, is for restoring function."[8] For example, during WWII, reconstructive surgery was advanced to repair faces destroyed by war wounds, to replace the less satisfactory use of rubber prostheses (masks) to cover the wounds.[9]

Among the purely reconstructive procedures we have observed lately are "full-face advancements" to correct genetic conditions such as Crouzon syndrome, a deforming condition occurring in early childhood, and full-face transplants to replace a damaged face. Crouzon syndrome is a "genetic condition in which the sutures of the skull and face fuse prematurely" creating an unusual countenance of bulgy eyes, protruding forehead, a pushed-in look to the middle face, and overly pronounced jaw.[10] It also poses health hazards such as compression of the tear ducts, inhibiting tears to flow, and restricted cranium space for a growing brain. The condition is relieved by cutting the bones of the face from the skull and attaching the bones to wires, which are then tightened with screws. The head is placed in a halo-like contraption that pulls at the sites of the fractures in a process of "full-face advancement," allowing the facial bones to grow and the face to move forward a millimeter per day until the face looks more "normal."

The first face transplant was conducted in 2005 to replace a damaged face with that of an undamaged face. A woman who lost her lips, part of her nose, and much of her lower face in an attack by her dog had the damaged part of her face replaced with a partial face transplant.[11] Since then, a multitude of face transplants have taken place, all for therapeutic purposes to correct massive disfigurement, rather than beauty enhancement. Much argued over by ethicists and surgeons, the use of full and partial face transplants is the replacement of a burned or mutilated face with a corpse's face, generating issues of identity. For instance, questions have been raised whether the transplant patient is a different person because she or he has someone else's face, whether the patient can adjust to adopting a dead or brain-dead person's parts, as well as the ethicality of using another person's body parts without preconsent. What is not at issue is the purpose, the correction of massive damage.[12]

The purpose for surgical procedures, medical or aesthetic, are not always so clear-cut. For example, gastric bypasses or stomach stapling, one might think, are purely medical. Some patients who undergo this procedure may be doing so under a physician's medical advice, in order to save the patients' lives. Yet some undergo the surgery for aesthetic reasons, as mentioned in the chapter on workplace and as illustrated by Deborah Voigt's weight loss surgery in order that she keep her job as an opera singer. Whatever the reason, some are so desperate to lose weight—for social, personal, and medical reasons—that they undergo these procedures at great cost, even at the risk of losing their lives.

Researchers at Harvard Medical School asked people to "imagine a treatment that would guarantee them an effortless weight loss." Given a range of risks they were willing to accept to lose weight, the respondents were asked if they would, for instance, be willing to risk death to achieve the weight loss. The researchers found that the heavier the respondent, the more she or he would risk death to lose weight. Startlingly, over half (52 percent) of overweight-to-obese respondents indicated they would risk death even for a piddling 10 percent weight loss. The study also found that many of the overweight-to-obese respondents "would give up some of their remaining years of life if they could live those years weighing slightly less.... almost any weight loss, even 10 percent, was something they longed for."[13] In less speculative terms, people actually do undergo bariatric surgery, making the choice between the risks associated with obesity (diabetes, heart disease, respiratory problems, and some forms of cancer) or the risks of significant complications or death from the weight-loss surgery.[14]

Surgery to Correct "Disabilities"

Here, let us consider the "medical model" or "disease model" as relevant to plastic surgery. In this model, the patient, the medical community, and possibly society at large consider some physical features as maladies in need of correction. Take the above paragraph on size-reduction surgery: the medical profession and the public, at least in part, seem to view extreme heaviness as a "problem" in need of surgical alteration. Certainly, we have firm evidence that other "ailments," such as small breasts and small penises, have been defined as disabilities and subject to surgery. An article published in *Plastic and Reconstructive Surgery* claimed for the first time (in 1950) that small breasts are a deformity, and this newly recognized "disability" was variously diagnosed "hypomastia" or "micromastia." Following this discovery of small breasts as a "disability" and the need for surgical remedies, the medical profession then pursued several decades of research and treatment for a similar "malady," which being the "small penis disease."[15] Thus, both women and men have undergone silicone injections and other enlargement procedures as "remedies." Small body parts are not the only pathology we find in need of correction. More broadly, since it affects all of us eventually, we "pathologize" aging. Looking old "is reworked into a medical riddle like smallpox or polio," requiring a "cure" for "symptoms" of aging.[16]

Demographics and Surgery

Gender. The American Society of Plastic Surgeons reports that it is mostly women (85–89 percent of roughly 7 million people) who get plastic surgery.[17] Although, increasingly men are undergoing cosmetic procedures, such as chest implants and facelifts, partly to impress romantic partners and partly to stay competitive in their work.[18] "Competition for corporate jobs among aging baby boomers, along with quicker, cheaper, and less invasive techniques and greater attention to grooming among men, are helping drive an increase in cosmetic procedures" among men. Women still outrank men in their increasing use of plastic surgery, with a 14 percent increase among women from 2002 to 2003 versus a 10 percent increase among men. But more frequently, men are getting nose jobs (currently the most popular surgical procedure among men), followed by eyelid surgery and liposuction. Much of striving for physical attractiveness is about competition and here we find a slight difference in the nature of the competition across genders: while men are concerned about staying competitive in the workplace, women reportedly compare themselves with unreachably beautiful fashion models.[19] I suspect that gender-surgery gaps will close as women become more involved in the labor market, especially at the professional levels. Women's needs for looking young and vibrant in the labor market will match men's needs; they have long surpassed men's needs to be attractive on a general level.

The gender gap wasn't always thus. Most of the late nineteenth century plastic surgery patients were men; in the twentieth century, aesthetic surgery came to be gendered female. More currently, the gender gap has been closing since the 1990s, with cosmetic surgery "approaching a time when it will not be gendered at all." Part of the explanation lies in the disappearing stigma of plastic surgery, with men becoming less sensitive to such stigma.[20]

Consider the percentage change in surgery frequency for women and men from 1997 to 2003: Botox injections have increased +3,177 percent for women and +5,762 percent for men, liposuction +117 percent for women and +118 percent for men, breast enlargement +177 percent for women, eyelid surgery +60 percent for women and +116 percent for men, nose reshaping +29 percent for women and +20 percent for men, breast reduction +207 percent for women and +97 percent for men, fat injections +141 percent for women and +86 percent for men, and hair transplants +71 percent for men.[21] Certainly, men are no strangers to surgical alterations but neither gender is receding from cosmetic surgery.

Race. Nineteenth-century cosmetic surgeons dealt with disfigurements that came from disease and war wounds. They also "tried to correct the 'ugliness' of nonwhite races."[22] They operated on ethnic (Irish, Jewish, Asian, and African) noses since these noses diverge from the Northern European standard of beauty.[23] They also fixed bat ears and jug ears thought to be common to the Irish. And of course they operated on the Asian eyelid (epicanthal) fold.

At the end of the nineteenth century, making the African nose appear more Caucasian became a concern of U.S. plastic surgeons. Beginning in the twentieth century, hair straightening and skin lightening became popular among African Americans attempting to "pass" as white, and plastic surgery in the 1940s and 1950s furthered passing even more.[24] Black became beautiful in the 1970s, when African Americans showed pride in a more natural physical appearance (such as natural, unstraightened hair) as well as African culture (music, clothing), African heritage, and so on. By the end of the twentieth century, the ideal among African Americans evolved into being not *too* visibly ethnic, to not look so black or so ethnic that it would discount one's chances of social success.[25] In the 1980s, for example, there was a shift to "ethnic-specific" cosmetic surgery such as lip-thinning and tip-flattening rhinoplasty as procedures of choice among African Americans. One "passed" in the latter twentieth century by looking like a whiter version of an African American, thus enabling greater economic and social power.[26]

During the Vietnam War, eyelid surgery (to achieve the double eyelid) and breast augmentations were very popular among Vietnamese women. After the U.S. withdrawal, a backlash occurred against Westernizing surgery, with such surgery virtually vanishing after 1975.[27] Now, in contemporary Vietnam, plastic surgery is back to Westernizing eyes as well as noses, increasing the size of noses to make them more European-looking. Similarly, in the post-Mao Tse-Tung People's Republic of China (PRC), there came an "explosion of interest in aesthetic surgery," mostly eyelid surgery. This explosion is partly due to increased wealth of the population (they could afford it) but largely because of the need to advance in one's career and to increase marriageability through a more Western appearance.[28]

However, Asian American women report that they undergo eyelid surgery not to appear more Caucasian per se, but to accrue the social and economic advantages of "more open, and hence more alert-seeming, eyes."[29]

Here's an interesting twist on changing oneself to be more acceptable to the majority race. Virginia Blum, author of a book on plastic surgery, underwent rhinoplasty, at her mother's direction, to rid herself of her Jewish nose. Though it wasn't her idea, the catalyst for the surgery was to marry well, specifically to marry a successful Jewish man. Yet, "it was just these Jewish men who, supposedly, were most desirous of the too-small imitation-WASP noses. In other words, our bodies weren't being honed and refashioned for a gentile market of prospective husbands. It was our own cultural and ethnic 'brothers' for whom we were being redesigned in the conventional WASP image."[30] Blum finds the same pattern among Asian American girls who undergo eyelid surgery, to achieve the Caucasian double lid, at the behest of their mothers. Eyelid surgery of these "Asian daughters is intended to appeal to the aesthetic taste of young Asian men, who presumably share the very racial traits they want changed."[31] So ethnic women alter their features for a more northern European appearance in order to appeal to their own ethnic partners, who share these same features. For that matter, both genders of nonwhite groups not uncommonly alter their appearance to advance themselves socially and economically. This is probably not some form of internal race hatred so much as it is knowing the score on what is considered physically attractive in the broader culture, a culture that has the power to offer and deny social advantages. It pays to look white.

Age. Aging is, of course, a major reason for plastic surgery. I noted as much in the above section on gender where it was reported that men, in order to retain their competitive edge, are increasingly undergoing rejuvenating surgeries. The ravages of age bias were described in the chapter on workplace (Chapter 3), demonstrating clearly that women, especially but not solely, are discriminated against as they age.

Cosmetic surgery to return the aging face and aging body to some semblance of youthfulness is fraught with issues of authentic versus inauthentic changes. Certainly we are under pressure to look as young as possible; yet, if discovered to have had, say, a facelift, our social audience will pass judgment on us all the same. As Sander Gilman, a noted expert on plastic surgery puts it, "If the cohort is able to detect the alteration . . . 'passing' becomes impossible."[32] Similarly, another writer finds that friends and family may have a very negative reaction to those who change themselves surgically, for example by facelifts, because they see the changes as deceptive, dishonest, and a misrepresentation of the self.[33] What a bind. If we want to gain social and economic advantages (jobs, romantic partners), we must surgically change ourselves. But to do so invites a different kind of stigma.

Yet the pressure persists. It not only persists but has become more prevalent, more pronounced, and more invading. More and more people are "age-dropping," a term used by Nancy Etcoff to describe the new pattern of starting youth-enhancing surgeries earlier in life, in our thirties rather than our fifties, with the idea being "never to visibly age at all."[34] Apparently, we need to begin our youth-generating surgeries earlier and have them more frequently.

Regional Differences. Different standards of beauty prevail in different parts of the world and even in different parts of the United States. Gluteal implants, implants to enlarge the buttocks, are far more popular in Brazil where protruding backsides are prized. Breast implants, by contrast, are much less popular in Brazil than in the United States, Europe, and Asia. Within the United States, there are clear regional variations, with distinct preferences for breast size. Women in the Sun Belt want larger breast implants than do women in the Northeast. Perhaps this is a difference in the need for subtlety, perhaps it is a difference in the type of attire usually worn allowing for greater and lesser exposure of the body.[35]

New Procedures

"Toe cleavage gains a foothold," says the subhead of a news article about seductive feet.[36] Most foot surgeries (80 percent) are corrective: to relieve bunions and claw (or hammer) toes that came about from squeezing toes into fashionable shoes. With increasing frequency, however, surgeons are performing delicate and expensive operations on women's feet (having toes lopped off and collagen implanted under the ball of the foot) *in order* that they may wear their favorite fashionable shoes.[37] Moreover, we are undergoing foot surgery not just to enable the wearing of high-fashion shoes but for foot beautification purposes, involving toes getting shortened or plumped and feet becoming narrowed. Women are having toe cleavage surgery to make the bare or scantily clad foot more sexually attractive.[38] This medically unnecessary surgery not infrequently costs as much as $12,000, or more. Toes are shortened at a cost of $2,500 per toe. Collagen injected into the balls of the feet to restore padding lost from years of wearing high heels costs about $500 per injection.[39]

Most podiatrists discourage foot-beautification surgeries because of the not-insignificant risk of permanent disability. But advocates for foot beautification procedures point out that critics of the surgery "simply do not understand the importance of high heels." As one advocate remarked, "Take your average woman and give her heels instead of flats, and she'll suddenly get whistles on the street," begging the question of why we would want to be whistled at.[40]

Another story about crippling lower extremities for aesthetic purposes is leg-lengthening surgery, as practiced in China. The cost of the surgery is about $6,000 to $7,000 for an added few inches of height. The long bones of the legs are broken and the legs are then placed in contraptions with plastic dials that the patients turn four times a day to winch their broken bones apart. The idea is that the gap between the broken bones will knit, the bones thus growing in length, taking over 2 weeks to elongate the bones less than half an inch. The patients usually are in the leg-lengthening device for 6 months followed by 3 more months in recovery. Yet, "Hundreds of young Chinese, more women than men, obsessed with stature in this increasingly crowded and competitive society, are stretching themselves to new heights." The risks are high. The legs can be of different lengths, they can be warped, and the knee and ankle joints can become deformed. The patient can be crippled for life if the bones are separated too quickly or if the bones grow together with tissue too fragile to bear the body's weight. Nerves are sometimes damaged. But, as we have seen with other hazardous behaviors that we engage in for cosmetic reasons, the purpose for engaging in leg-lengthening surgery, as reported by those who undergo it, is to be competitive on the job market, to gain college entrance, and to attract an advantageous marriage.[41]

Onto less gruesome surgeries, let us now consider a new way of hair restoration. In a process mostly used by men, instead of the old-fashioned method of taking tufts (plugs) of hair from one's own body and transferring them to the head, individual hair follicles are transplanted. In the new technique, whole strips of hair, including the skin, are removed from the back of the head (where the hair is more plentiful) and individual follicles are painstakingly planted into the bald spots. This new method removes the artificial ("doll's hair") appearance of the hair plugs, giving forth a natural-looking crop of hair.[42] Women are engaging in a similar hair transplant procedure with the recent use of eyelash transplants. Actually, eyelash transplants have been around for over 10 years but were used solely for burn victims who lost their lashes. Lately, healthy patients have been receiving lash transplants for purely cosmetic reasons. In the same manner as described above with men's hair transplants, hair and follicles are removed from the back of the scalp and implanted in the eyelid. Aside from the usual risks (infection, etc.), the new lashes require frequent trimming (since hair from the head grows) and curling (since eyelashes must curl away from the eye).[43]

Another new procedure, one that has not been met with much satisfaction, is penis enlargement surgery. In fact, the rate of dissatisfaction is quite high, over 70 percent. The reasons have to do with unrealistic expectations: the average increase in length is 1.3 centimeters (half an inch) and misbegotten ideas about the importance of a large penis (for which the surgeons suggest counseling would pay off better than surgery).[44] With penis transplants, sometimes the patient and significant others are dissatisfied with the new organs. A victim of an accident underwent a successful penis transplant. The results were perfect, blood flow was good, and the penis could be used for urination and for intercourse. But the man and his wife had severe psychological problems with it and the transplanted penis had to be cut off. This is not uncommon for other transplanted parts as well (hands, etc.) with the recipient growing mentally detached from the new body part.[45]

Facelifts have been updated. Basically, the facelift, not a new procedure, has utilized the same techniques for about a century. To vastly oversimplify, the facelift involves cuts behind and in front of the ears, the facial muscles are smoothed out, the excess skin is then pulled taut, the loose skin is removed, and the incisions are sutured up. But now we are being convinced that we need early and frequent facelifts, and these facelifts need not be so drastic. A new procedure uses "barbed sutures," which enables the surgeon to insert tiny barbs under the skin using only small incisions, to pull the skin up and taut. Recovery takes only days rather than weeks, and the surgery is far less invasive. We also now have injectable fillers, allowing surgeons to inject natural substances, such as the patient's own fat, to fill out the wrinkly parts of the face (brow, smile lines, and the lips). Another new technique, facial implants, involve molded silicone implants, unlike silicone gel used for breast implants, which are inserted in various parts of the face, notably the chin or cheekbones. Such implants can also be inserted into other parts of the body, such as the calves of the legs.[46]

Liposuction, a new-ish technique of vacuuming fat from the body, may be the single most common surgical procedure in the world.[47] Liposuction, by the way, is a permanent solution only for problem areas, like thick ankles or "jodhpur thighs" on otherwise thin people. Heavy people who undergo liposuction will regain the fat unless their lifestyles (diet and exercise) are altered. Lately, liposuction has become "a tool to enhance the near-perfect body parts of the already fit." Its new role, to perfect the already almost perfect, has replaced its previous role of reducing flabby hips, thighs, and abdomens. A plastic surgeon who offers this method of perfection describes his patients as "perfect 10s who want to be $10\frac{1}{2}$s."[48]

Liposuction is not an effective treatment for cellulite, the pockets of uneven fat under the skin giving forth an orange-peel appearance.[49] Thus far, nothing seems to eliminate or reduce cellulite even though dermatologists have tried melting cellulite with lasers, spa technicians have tried breaking it apart with vigorous massage, and cosmetics manufacturers sell creams and gels to reduce its appearance. Enter "mesotherapy," a newly devised and questionable technique to reduce cellulite. Mesotherapy is a method of injecting a cocktail of medicines and other substances into the mesoderm, the layer of fat and connective tissue under the skin where cellulite resides, hoping to dissolve the fat. The procedure has been in use in France for over 50 years, but has only recently been made available in the United States. Does it work? A doctor who applies the procedure says, not surprisingly, that it does. There is, however, no empirical evidence that it does work; we only have "hearsay and unsubstantiated clinical findings." As with all surgical procedures there are risks, in this case bacterial infections, sores, and scarring. The cost is usually less than liposuction, which can start at $5000 per procedure. Mesotherapy can cost from $900 to $15,000 for six to ten sessions.[50]

Homogenizing Our Looks through Surgery

So we come full circle from the beginning of this chapter, in which I mentioned the growing acceptance of plastic surgery and the growing numbers of people undergoing it. We, in the United States especially, have a ready acceptance of plastic surgery. Some individuals have numerous (over 20) cosmetic surgeries by the time they're in the early 30s. It is reported that, on one day alone, a 32-year-old women had a "breast implant exchange; liposuction to her flanks, hips, thighs, and abdomen; a modified brow lift; lip augmentation; and a graft of fat into her cheeks." Surgery recipients flaunt their surgeries on Web sites and among their friends.

The stigma is gone. Partly, the TV reality shows like "Extreme Makeover" serve as the catalyst for such broad social acceptance of plastic surgery. More far-reaching explanations include (a) the technological advances that have made cosmetic surgery safer and have lessened recovery time, (b) the financial costs have been reduced to within reach of the middle class, and (c) an increasing dissatisfaction with one's appearance. More of us see things about ourselves that we don't like, supposedly unattractive "defects" that may be imagined or are greatly exaggerated. About half of

United States women and men are unhappy with their looks, our unhappiness at least partly spawned by our exposure to mass media images of beauty. These images with which we compare ourselves are themselves artificial: the images are not uncommonly computer enhanced and, even when the images reflect genuinely beautiful people, those beautiful people are a tiny minority of human beings. The great majority of us do not look like them and never will regardless of how much surgery we have (or how much we diet, apply cosmetics, etc.). Yet we are unhappy with our looks anyway and, if we are convinced that cosmetic surgery is safe and we can afford it, we go for it.[51]

Because we, as a population, are increasingly using plastic surgery to perfect ourselves and to more closely resemble beautiful icons, we are increasingly becoming similar in our looks. The chin implants, the brow lifts, and other alterations make us look alike.[52] The "current obsession with plastic surgery ... has turned Beauty into a kind of physiological sameness." This trend is not new or unique to plastic surgery since so many of the changes we put ourselves through in the hopes of becoming more attractive (cosmetics, diets, girdles, and so on) mold us into some ideal, widely accepted, agreed-upon, standardized form of "beauty."[53] We can refer to our surgical homogenization as "cookie-cutter plastic surgery." If the times and the culture dictate that women must have large breasts or particularly shaped breasts, no problem. (One author points out that in the 1950s, we were interested in pointed breasts, the popular breasts of the 1980s were softer and bigger, and in the 1990s and now, we prefer large, muscular breasts.) We get our ideas about how we should look from interactive relationships between cultural icons, such as celebrities, and plastic surgeons. As members of the ordinary public, we enforce the beauty standards when we ask the surgeons to make us into the cultural icons that we so admire.[54]

Homogenization of beauty overlaps with the democratization of beauty in an obvious way. If we adhere to the same beauty standards—for example, if we want high cheek bones—we can have them if plastic surgery becomes available and within the financial means of so many of us. Democratization of beauty has occurred largely because costs of cosmetic surgery have declined, thus narrowing the distance between those who can afford to look young and attractive, formerly a sign of privilege, and those who are the unretouched and naturally beautiful. At the same time, with the increasing use of beautifying surgery, the gap has widened between the attractive, who are increasingly plentiful, and the plain.[55] If attractive people are commonplace, however, one wonders whether plain people will be the subject of even greater bias.

The Many Forms of and Reasons for Surgery: A Summary

Cross-culturally, we have engaged in some "bizarre and grotesque methods of gross physical manipulation" including the practices of clitoridectomy, foot-binding, and the removal of bones to fit into the tight corsets.[56] A minority take matters into our own hands, changing ourselves without the benefit of established medical treatment, via scarification. Scarification may be thought of as self-surgery or informal surgery. Those who engage in it are called "delicate self-cutters" and are most often adolescent females who cut their skin when experiencing grave anxiety. The self-cutters make shallow, carefully wrought cuts across skin, sometimes in the form of parallel lines and sometimes in intricate patterns of flowers, circles, or rectangles. The self-cutters make these self-inflicted "corrections" defiantly and unguiltily.[57] In an intriguing turn of logic, William Saletan forces us to question how self-mutilation is less rational than other forms of body modification such as Botox injections, liposuction, and circumcision. Because self-mutilation is a more informal method of altering our appearance doesn't mean that it is more questionable than, say, surgically "correcting" sexually ambiguous infants, often with disastrous results. Saletan's point is that it is a matter of relativity: what we see as normal, acceptable procedures to change our appearance is not remotely different from what we see as abnormal and unacceptable procedures.[58] With or without formalized surgical tools and training, we feel the need to change our looks. And we do. We will probably always, and in all cultures, make physical changes to ourselves.

Bodies and faces are not coherent, unidimensional, or permanent, but instead are changing and transitory. Think of the aging body, or the fattening or thinning body, or the unhealthy versus the healthy body. We as societal members, subject to social judgment, experience self-dissatisfaction when we fail to achieve unchanging bodies, when our bodies grow wider or saggier. Our dissatisfaction is met with the knowledge that our faces and bodies are subject to change, adaptable, and customizable by surgical and other interventions.[59] Our physical beings can be thought of as "cultural plastic."[60] The body has the potential for limitless change and can continuously be modified and upgraded in accordance with social dictates.[61]

Whether we *should* undergo these changes, succumb to the pressure to change ourselves, is the unanswered, subjective, and personal question.

PART 3

The System

CHAPTER 7

The Medical and Health Insurance Communities

Health insurance doesn't ordinarily cover looks-improvement procedures, making medical practice as related to such procedures highly lucrative and hassle free for the medical practitioners engaging in it. Because it is not covered by health insurance, it is usually out of reach for the economically deprived who need it for getting good jobs and for otherwise improving their lives.

Never mind cosmetic procedures for the moment because, in our culture, health insurance and medical care is quite limited for legitimate, noncosmetic medical needs, making health maintenance and preventive care scarce or nonexistent. In a typical Catch-22 situation, we also know that legitimate medical care is dependent upon what we look like in addition to being dependent on whether we have health insurance or upon our ability to pay. Those of us with undesirable appearance traits are more likely to receive substandard care.

Double standards abound in dental care, for example, depending upon the patient's appearance and socioeconomic level. "In a nation where a person's smile is considered a sign of general well-being and an important factor in landing a job, dental care is becoming ever more unequal," and the problem is worsening.[1] People with money can have "movie star smiles" whereas people without are more likely to have bad or missing teeth.[2] Short people also face more health problems than do taller people. Again, the reason lies in the double-edged sword: living a socioeconomically disadvantaged life, due to having a lesser job because one is short, leads to increased health risks. We already know from the chapter on workplace that short men earn less income than taller men; we now learn that they pay a price in overall health and health care because they are short.[3]

There are also troublesome clashes between categories of people, such as the disabled and the heavy, and the medical community. Differences of opinion exist between the disabled and the medical community on fundamental values, such as the value of life and the financial cost of well being. More specifically, the disabled face a range of medical issues including appropriate treatment, health care access, costs of health care, health care rationing, and even assisted suicide, with these issues often in conflict with each other. Medical definitions themselves as they pertain to disability, such as what constitutes work disability and major activity limitation, are entangled by issues of *source* of the pathology. That is, the medical community and not uncommonly the broader society views the pathology as residing solely within disabled individuals whereas the disabled and thoughtful members of society recognize that societally created factors, external to the disabled, limit the health care afforded to the disabled as well as limiting disabled people's ability to perform "expected" social roles.[4] Some of these same conflicts arise in the consideration of medical treatment of the heavy, notably the costs of care and the internalized versus externalized blame for the health problems associated with size. Looks bias as it affects health and health care is indeed quite pronounced when we consider weight and its effect on medical care and insurance coverage.

Health Care, Health Insurance, and Size

The medical profession's philosophy and practice as related to body size, based on insurance standards, have changed greatly over the decades. With the nineteenth century came the quantification of fat (as measured in pounds) as an indicator of health, and thus, the possibility of *ranking* pounds/health ratios. These pounds/health ratios were displayed in a table of "differences," exhibiting ranges in weight across a population. In other words, people can be placed on a hierarchy of healthy versus not-healthy depending upon their comparative weight, whether or not their weight is validly related to their health. By the 1860s, insurance companies developed height-and-weight charts linking size to mortality, depending upon where a person was "positioned within a hierarchy, according to . . . differences from a hypothetical average."[5] Two standards for determining weight as a health problem were eventually devised: the Body Mass Index and the Metropolitan Life Insurance Company Height and Weight Tables.[6]

Numerical charts used by insurance companies, which appear to be inarguable, have been discovered to be not so inarguable. If such numerical indices were inarguable, they would not have changed over time, but they have. In the mid-twentieth century, weight tables and calorie charts were altered from their formerly "traditional" standards, when we found that "acceptable levels of one decade were denounced as lax in the next."[7] As a result, acceptable weight levels were lowered by Metropolitan Life Insurance. For example, "standardized" weight tables reduced their weight standards by around 8 percent in a 17-year period (1942–1959), meaning that we were expected to weigh less, in order to be considered healthy, in the later time period than in previous time periods.[8] In all of these measures of weight/health, the artificiality of the standards themselves is the one element that remains stable. The mere fact of altering standards across time begs the question of whether weight as an indicator of health can be agreed upon and knowable, whether we can state categorically that x number of pounds per inches of height means healthy or not healthy. By the twentieth century, the pretense of purely medical concerns about body weight was overshadowed by a perhaps more genuine interest in fat reduction: money.[9]

The Costs

Changes in medical and insurance definitions of health, and the related social attitudes about health, affect the cost of health and life insurance. As just mentioned, based on health insurance companies' labeling of acceptable and unacceptable weight, heavy people can be forced to pay more for their insurance. The insurance label of "morbid obesity" is not a diagnosis, writes a leading figure in the fat-acceptance movement, it is discrimination, with heavy people having to pay as much as four times for health insurance as thinner people, if they can get health insurance at all.[10]

Nonetheless, the heavy are often forced to pay greater insurance costs related to obesity. It is reported that, "Treating obesity-related disorders costs as much or more than illnesses caused by aging, smoking, and problem drinking." If it is true that being overweight increases the chances of diabetes, cardiovascular disease, osteoarthritis, and so on, people who aren't heavy may feel cheated when paying increased healthcare premiums, since they are not personally at risk, in the same way as they would if they pay more for their premiums to cover the risky behaviors of smokers and drinkers if they, personally, don't smoke or drink. A 2006 survey of over 1,500 Americans, as reported in *Health Affairs*, demonstrates that most of the respondents feel that people who engage in "irresponsible" behaviors, such as smoking and overeating, should pay for their "unhealthy behavior." Sixty percent of the respondents favor higher insurance premiums for smokers and 30 percent felt that the obese should pay more for insurance.[11]

However, to a significant degree, healthcare spending on obesity-related problems is due to prescription drug costs and hospital stays. If the reports are accurate that obese patients require more medication for diabetes, cardiovascular disease, pain relief, asthma, and other illnesses than people with a lower weight, the overall health care costs are due to the usurious price of pharmaceuticals. So, to the extent that we are being cheated in our healthcare costs, we may more appropriately look to the pharmaceutical companies and insurance corporations as the source.[12]

Part of the rationalization of higher health insurance premiums is the view that heavy people *can* control their weight and they *ought to*. These differential costs would be explainable and acceptable if we knew for certain that weight/health ratios were valid. Instead, confusion reigns in the changing insurance standards and in the changing medical findings about the weight/health nexus, as we found in Chapter 1. There are caveats to both arguments—that "fat-and-fit" is no less healthy than thin-and-unfit versus fat is never a healthy state—leaving us to question the appropriateness of health insurance denial and health insurance overcharging.

Causality, Fault, and Remedies

As a society we have changed our minds about the healthiness, physical appeal, and other traits associated with weight, having once thought fat was a sign of health, prosperity, fertility, and beauty. More recently, and by 1990 particularly, the medical community and the broader culture began to view obesity as a character defect, as a self-control problem, with some physicians beginning to express disdain toward obese patients.[13] As a legal advocate for the weight-discriminated puts it, the basic beliefs held by the medical community about body weight include: fat is unhealthy, body size is volitional, weight is mutable, and weight loss is a benign procedure.[14]

As to causality, one point of view backed by research, is that body size is genetic and thus "forgivable," while another common but unsubstantiated viewpoint is that body size is totally within one's control. Although some medical practitioners have a genuine concern for the health of their heavy patients, clearly some in the medical community display no understanding toward people-of-size. "Fat Equals Lazy" is the title of a report finding that "doctors are guilty of wrongly believing that obese people are simply lazy."[15]

As to treatment of obesity, it will remain a matter of opinion whether the overweight should try to lose weight through surgery, diet, and exercise or, conversely, whether society should adopt a more accepting attitude about body size. Since we are still in the cultural stage of not accepting people of various sizes, it can be assumed that the common public and medical opinion is that we need to treat obesity by (a) reducing it and (b) treating medical conditions associated with obesity.

These questions, though not fully dissected, are extremely important ones to resolve because medical care depends upon views about obesity. If, for instance, doctors view obesity as a lack of self control, and if society sees similarities between obesity and other stigmatized health statuses (alcoholism and smoking), we can anticipate that doctors, insurance corporations, and the public will lack sympathy for the obese. We can further expect health insurance companies to refuse to insure heavy people or force them to pay enormous health insurance costs. We can expect the medical community to be unwilling to treat the obese or to be insensitive to their needs. When this happens, the obese tend not to seek preventive treatment for acute illness, illnesses that then become chronic and deadly.[16]

Biases in Prevention and Treatment

"When people realize that they can't get away with expressing their prejudice against fat outright, they use the health argument instead."[17] In the fat-acceptance perspective, the health argument is a smokescreen for fat hatred. Where the weight/health argument does have validity is in the reluctance to seek preventive medical attention because one is overweight. Not only do heavy people have difficulty getting health insurance, they are reluctant to face the humiliation and lectures from medical practitioners. Regardless of the presenting symptoms (viruses, etc.) or regardless of the patients' preventive checkup needs, doctors often interject their concerns about the patient's weight rather than the reason for the appointment.[18] Women-of-size are at increased risk compared to thinner women for breast, cervical, endometrial, and ovarian cancer. But they are a third less likely to get routine preventive care, such as breast exams, gynecological exams, and pap smears for cervical cancer because they have faced size stigma in the past by medical professionals.[19]

In the medical treatment of heavy people, those who do want to lose weight find themselves in a real dilemma since prohibitive health insurance costs may prevent their seeking weight loss treatment. In a report about insurers balking at the cost and risk of bariatric surgeries, we find that insurers can deny approval for surgeries even with doctors' letters stating that medical reasons make these surgeries imperative.[20] Complications, including heart attacks and strokes, from bariatric surgery are serious for one out of twenty bariatric surgery patients. Five percent of bariatric patients experience serious cardiovascular difficulties, post-surgery. The mortality rate for gastric bypass, the most common type of bariatric surgery, is 1 in 200. All this adds up to risk of malpractice lawsuits against doctors and hospitals, and great reluctance of health plans to cover bariatric surgery. Some malpractice insurers have dropped bariatric coverage altogether, and some surgeons have stopped performing the surgery rather than pay the sharply higher malpractice insurance premiums. Most of us cannot afford to pay cash for the surgery since bariatric procedures cost an average of $25,000; with complications, the bill can come to over $100,000.[21] So people needing and wanting this surgery are not getting it.

Positive Medical News

On a more positive note, we find that super-sized medical care, at least the physical elements of it, has proliferated. Because the proportion of larger people is increasing, industries that make and sell medical supplies and equipment for the larger body have boomed. Among the plus-size medical equipment now available are: longer injection needles, larger blood-pressure cuffs, wheelchairs up to 4 feet wide, scales that measure over 600 pounds, hospital beds sturdy enough to not collapse under larger amounts of weight, "ample-wear" gowns, armless love seats in waiting rooms, sturdy and large examination tables, and super-sized imaging (for instance MRI) machines.[22] Strictly medically speaking, this seems like a step in the correct direction given the embarrassment that heavy people face when seeking medical care and given that heavy people, like people of all sizes, need adequate medical care. Without such innovations like longer injection needles, medicine cannot reach the target (for example, the buttocks muscles), and some diagnostic procedures (like MRIs) simply can't be done.

The Future

Our immediate future in the United States does not look promising regarding affordable health care. We can expect a continued absence of dental and medical care, available and affordable to all, and this absence affects not only our health but also our appearance. Our appearance, in turn, affects the health care we receive or are denied.

Much of this book is about inequality and bias. Let me close this chapter with a new method of discrimination against people based on their physical attributes. Many countries already have amassed huge data banks of DNA information about their publics. This information has a number of nefarious functions, one being to deny health insurance or make health insurance premiums very costly. Internationally, the insurance community considers genetic information its newest priority, with insurers increasingly subsuming genetic traits under "pre-existing conditions."[23] "Insurance discrimination" is "genetic discrimination" when someone is denied coverage or is forced to pay increased premiums because of genetically-determined preexisting conditions.[24] From this, we might foresee a future in which a "cross-referenced genetic information bureau would permit insurers and financial institutions to create a commercial 'genetic underclass.'"[25] I wonder if various physical features, such as obesity, poor teeth, shortness, crooked spines, poor eyesight requiring corrective lenses or surgery, skin disorders, and other undesirable traits would be considered preexisting conditions and thus "valid" (read: explainable) reasons for denial of health insurance. These and other appearance-related conditions can be and sometimes are met with medical attention when those needing this attention are insured. For this reason, health insurers are likely opposed to their continued coverage.

In sum, medical conditions that pose health and aesthetic disadvantages may cause us to be denied medical care. At least some appearance-related traits, such as body mass, are recorded for insurance purposes and these traits can be the basis for medical and insurance bias.

CHAPTER 8

The Legal Community

"Ultimately, you can't change the world through litigation. You have to change the hearts and minds and the culture," so says Paul Steven Miller, a law professor at the University of Washington.[1] He was mentioned in Chapter 3 on workplace as someone who had experienced job discrimination due to his dwarfism. Eventually, he did get a good job at a renowned university and, importantly, his abilities are recognized by his students, fellow faculty, and all who work with him. Professor Miller is correct that, through exposure to wide ranges of people, awareness is raised. With exposure and awareness, bias can then change to acceptance. This would be true for people who do not fit the social strictures of physical appearance the same as it has been true for minorities. Realistically, these changes he mentions—changes in hearts, and minds, and culture—though necessary, are much more difficult and more time-consuming than litigation. Unfortunately, at times we must resort to legal strategies to seek enforced equality.

People are discriminated against on the basis of their appearance. If we are old, unattractive, heavy, short, disfigured, non-Aryan, and so on, we may experience bias in the workplace, bias in access (maneuvering through physical structures, such as buildings, public transportation, and airline seating), and bias in housing. The more informal forms of bias, in which we may be excluded from important social networks (marriage, friendships, etc.), are less amenable to legal action even though their consequences are equally significant.

Employment Discrimination

First, let us tackle appearance discrimination in employment. You may recall from Chapter 3 the less-than-young woman who lost her job at a cosmetics counter because she was not "hot." You may also recall Abercrombie and Fitch's policy to hire only young, attractive, white salespeople. Recall furthermore, the case of the woman denied a manager's position at McDonald's because of a facial disfigurement. We might think that, as time passes and as societies progress on equal rights, we would not be troubled by looks discrimination. Clearly that has not entirely been the case. Naomi Wolf reminds us that while the feminist movement "gave us laws against job discrimination based on gender; immediately case law evolved in Britain and the United States that institutionalized job discrimination based on women's appearance."[2] Meaning: as soon as it was no longer legal to discriminate on the basis of gender (or race, age, and so on), we found a way to discriminate on gender (and other minority traits) via appearance.

This is precisely the juncture at which employers have been subject to discrimination suits. Title VII, a federal law protecting against disparate treatment by employers based on race, color, religion, gender, or national origin, does not specifically rule against unfair employment decisions because of a person's size. But it does disallow "illegal discrimination *based on characteristics that are protected by Title VII*" such as the above-mentioned race, color, religion, gender, and national origin.[3] While weight is not provided any "direct protection" in discrimination cases, it can be a protected category because there is a correlation between weight and ethnicity (with African Americans and Hispanics having a higher incidence of obesity), age (with older people more likely to be heavier than younger people), and gender (with women being subject to more stringent standards of weight than men). So, cases of illegal discrimination against the weighty can be made if nonwhite, older, and female workers are treated unfairly because of their weight.[4]

Experimental studies show that "weight-related standards are not applied consistently to men and women." Moreover, "women are judged more harshly for being overweight, and those judgments influence employment-related decisions [and there is] a consistent differential effect of weight on the wages of men and women."[5] Continental Airlines was successfully sued when it was determined that the airline's weight restrictions applied more stringently to female flight attendants than to male flight attendants (*Gerdom v. Continental Airlines, Inc.* 1982). Here it was found that it "was not merely slenderness, but slenderness of female employees, which the employer considered critical."[6] Similarly, the now-defunct Pan

Am Airlines lost its case when it was determined that weight policies were enforced against female flight attendants and not enforced against male flight attendants, while both genders were supposed to be equally subject to weight standards (*Union of Flight Attendants v. Pan American World Airways, Inc.* 1987).[7] In the *Wong-Larkin v. United Airlines, Inc.* (1996) case, United Airlines lost on the basis of gender *and* age discrimination. United made the argument that weight restrictions hold regardless of age. But flight attendants succeeded in establishing adjusted base maximum weights depending on age, allowing for added weight as age increases.[8]

The airlines are hardly alone in looks discrimination. Jennifer Portnick demands that she be judged "only on what I can do" and won an employment discrimination case against the Jazzercise Company to that effect. Ms. Portnick had asked for a franchise from Jazzercise Inc., where she was to be a Jazzercise instructor, but was rejected for being too plump.[9] She won, relying on the "fat ordinance" passed in San Francisco in 2000, to be discussed in a moment. British teenager Emma Hall did not have similar luck. She passed her job interview with Virgin Trains, but was later told that she couldn't have the job after all because she is too heavy. She responded that, regardless of Virgin Train's image consciousness, she is physically sound and capable of doing the work. Virgin Trains decided that attractiveness outweighs the health and capability of the employee.[10]

In a touch of irony, a purveyor of high-fat food, McDonald's, refused to hire a man because he's overweight. Joseph Connor filed a lawsuit in 2002 against McDonald's claiming that McDonald's violated the Fair Employment Practices Act and the Americans with Disabilities Act (ADA) when they refused to hire him because of his weight. Mr. Connor, who weighs 420 pounds, was determined to be morbidly obese in McDonald's judgment and thus not employable. McDonald's has argued that obesity is not a "physical impairment" and therefore not protected by the ADA, unless it is the result of a physiological disorder.[11]

Other Forms of Discrimination

Landlords sometimes refuse to rent to people-of-size, while they have no qualms about renting to thin applicants.[12] There is a conspicuous absence of laws to protect against such bias. One state, Michigan, includes the word "weight" in its civil rights legislation. And three local ordinances in Santa Cruz, California, San Francisco, and Washington, DC, prohibit discrimination in employment, housing, and public accommodations based on physical traits. Washington, DC, is the only place that specifically forbids discrimination based on any appearance traits.[13]

The most recent passage of a "fat ordinance" was on May 8, 2000, in San Francisco, legally prohibiting discrimination against people based on their size. The San Francisco ordinance is distinct from the few other such ordinances because it also applies to thin people and people of various heights, thus broadening the meaning of size as a discriminatory factor. Fat-acceptance advocates say the ordinance is "a necessary remedy for all those who have ever been insulted, denied a seat at a restaurant, or been rejected for a job because of their appearance." The manner in which San Francisco went about this legislation is instructive and could be used as a helpful guideline for future ordinances in other cities or, for that matter, on state and federal levels. Borrowing from previous civil rights litigation, the San Francisco measure has added height and weight to the same antidiscrimination codes that provide protections for people based on race, religion, color, ancestry, age, gender, sexual orientation, disability, and place of birth.[14]

One of the latest focal points for size discrimination has been airline seating, most obvious in Southwest Airline's policy of charging people-of-size for two seats if they have difficulty fitting into one. The airlines have a variety of different policies, some more restrictive than others.[15] But the upshot is that people-of-size can be denied boarding if they cannot fit into one seat and cannot afford to pay for an additional one. On Southwest flights, if passengers-of-size are flying on a full airplane or one near-capacity, they must pay double of what another person would pay if they cannot squeeze between the armrests or if they need seatbelt extensions. While Southwest Airline's seating policy has received the most notoriety of late, the extra-seat policy is not unique to Southwest. American Airlines has a similar policy requiring the purchase of an extra seat if the passengers' bodies protrude over into the adjacent seat. It doesn't take much of a mental leap to understand why the airlines install very small coach seats; obviously, the more people they can fit into each flight, the more money they make. Corporate desire for profit takes precedence over the physical comfort of the passengers to the point of making even medium-sized people uncomfortable in ordinary coach seats. By the way, it is not only heavy people who struggle in airline seating. Tall people do also. And it's not just tall and heavy people who suffer; smaller people suffer when they get crushed by a large seatmate. The problem seems to be the size of the seats rather than the size of the people.

The row caused by airlines charging heavy people an extra fee for two airline seats has been a source of major complaint not only because of the unfairness of charging extra money based on a physical trait but also because of the discretion applied by the airline decision makers. Other carriers besides Southwest and American have informal, or formal, but always discretionary, policies on the extra seat requirement. While the criterion of fitting between the armrests seems objective enough, it is not uncommon that customer service representatives (gate agents) and flight attendants make the judgment on whether a passenger requires two seats even if she or he can fit between the armrests.

There are a number of issues—legal, economic, and possibly occupational—related to size, access, and the legalities of denying people airplane seats. It may be a work issue if people can't fly at the same cost as smaller people to work-related activities such as meetings. A large businessman (6 feet 9 inches in height and 400 pounds in weight) says he travels in first class as frequently as possible. But this solution has no meaning for most of us who cannot afford first class.[16] A businesswoman-of-size was removed from a flight because of her size, even though the seatbelt fastened around her, the armrest slid down without a problem, and she only needed one seat. Nonetheless, she was asked to purchase the seat next to her. She refused to pay or to leave, was instructed to get off the flight, and is now suing Southwest Airlines.[17]

The President of the Air Travelers Association has commented that he supports charging heavy people ("certain people" he called them) for two seats out of fairness to the other passengers. "If people are taking up two seats," he said, "they ought to pay for two seats. They really are impinging on the sense of fairness."[18] Airlines do receive complaints from passengers who report that their seating was encroached upon by larger seatmates and that they have been "sat on" during their flights. Virgin Atlantic Airline has paid a passenger almost $21,000 for damages sustained from being "squashed" by a seatmate-of-size on a transatlantic flight. The passenger suffered a blood clot in her chest, torn leg muscles, and acute sciatica and, years later, is still in pain.[19] A heavy passenger injuring a not-heavy passenger indeed poses a dilemma. The airline in this case paid damages to the now permanently disabled plaintiff. In large part, this seems a fair remedy since it can be effectively argued that the airline is at fault for cramming as much "revenue" as possible into the airplane.

Summary

We can only guess that most cases of looks-based bias go unchallenged. If we are denied jobs, housing, seating, and so on because of our looks, the reason may be unstated (we're told we're not qualified, for example) or, if we do reject the explanation as viable, our legal system is reluctant to take the case to its ultimate, fair-minded conclusion. Recall the "ugly laws" mentioned in the Introduction. These statutes prohibited "unsightly beggars" (mainly the diseased, maimed, and otherwise disabled) from appearing in city streets in a number of U.S. cities from 1867 to 1974. They were never met with legal challenges. The laws died on their own due to a lack of enforcement but not because their legality was questioned.[20]

Appearance does influence employment decisions, housing options, physical access, and so on although there seems to be no immediately justifiable, legal explanation for it. Having reviewed the evidence, a general statement can be made that physical features (size, skin texture, "beauty," skin color, eye shape, etc.), are mostly a matter of factors beyond our control, as is true for demographic statuses for which we cannot legally be discriminated against.

Another matter almost completely beyond our control is social class, the subject of the next chapter. As we have discovered throughout this book, many of us are not economically advantaged; and being poor or working-poor ensures that we do not have the resources for dental care, hair dressing, and so on. Maybe choice plays a role in some features of our appearance. But mostly, we do not choose to be physically unattractive and most of us do everything we can to be as presentable as possible. We know the consequences of not being attractive and they are not pleasant.

CHAPTER 9

The Economy, Globalization, and Power

As with probably all things in the present day, the economy is global and so are the economic issues relevant to physical appearance. Beauty has become globalized, such that mostly we are all subject to the same standards. This standardized beauty is relevant to the economy in that, as Naomi Wolf summarizes, "'Beauty' is a currency system like the gold standard."[1] We can take this to mean that beauty is a commodity, a form of capital, whose value we mostly agree upon.

Let us here reconsider global standards of physical attractiveness. Looks standards, you may recall from the Introduction to this book, have become homogenized, globally, as white Northern European. This has wreaked havoc for the peoples of the world who do not have white Northern European features since they are pressured, if they wish to be economically and socially successful, to be tall, slim, light-colored in skin and hair, and with Aryan facial structure.

Beauty is universal, as has been amply documented at this point in human history. That is, attractiveness ratings are remarkably consistent, with "people in the same culture [agreeing] strongly about who is beautiful and who is not."[2] Allow me to offer two noteworthy examples of intracultural agreement on beauty, which are opposed to global agreement about beauty, by way of pointing out the significance of just how homogenized our standards of beauty are. While most other cultures exert enormous pressure on women to be thin, a very few size-generous cultures adore women who are soft and fleshy. Surprisingly, Brazil, the home of supermodels exported worldwide, intraculturally considers plumpness beautiful and sexy, with the idealized feminine form being guitar-shaped, with a smallish bust and waist and ample, fleshy hips. Indeed, Sander Gilman refers to this unexpected occurrence (supermodels exported but fleshy women revered at home) as the "Brazilian Mix and Match," and displays the silicone implants for the buttocks used to round out the derrieres of Brazilian women.[3] In South Africa, slimness is thought to be a sign of illness. Here, "a hefty girth has long been a sign of well-being and a slim woman is the subject of nasty gossip."[4] These exceptions to global standards are virtually alone, thus accentuating their exceptionality: by virtue of their distinction, they prove the rule. The more global ideal, prevalent in the rest of the world (notably, the United States, Europe, and Asia), is thinness, clearly emphasized, especially in women, as a sign of beauty.

In addition to globalized beauty standards and variances of those standards, the global and local economies influence not only our worldwide beauty standards but also (a) the things we do to change our appearance as well as (b) patterns of consumption (of food, clothing, etc.) having to do with our appearance. In this chapter we will see that the profit motive determines the size of our bodies and, significantly, the goods and services accommodating our increased size. Socioeconomic class issues pertinent to size and beauty shape our appearance by determining the services and products we can buy to improve our appearance. And, the overall health of the economy can determine the goods and services available to us and purchasable by us. Converging with the economy and globalization is the profit motive of the U.S. food industry, looming with health hazards and visiting itself not just on the U.S. populace. The profit motive and the health consequences are, unhappily, exported to other cultures.

The Food Industry

Food production in the United States, as well as eating practices (eating in fast food restaurants) and the food itself (convenient, high-fat and high-sugar food) have spread throughout the world, literally changing the shape of people while endangering their health.

Fatty and plentiful western food, such as spam, has turned Micronesians into Macronesians, "taking a disastrous toll on people in developing countries."[5] This New World Syndrome is bringing with it diabetes, heart disease, hypertension, vascular breakdown, renal failure, and high blood pressure, which have become greater medical problems than the traditional problems of infectious diseases. Hugely increased body size and related medical problems have soared globally but especially among "peoples in transition—Polynesians, Native Americans, and aboriginal Australians; Asian Indian emigrants to Fiji, South Africa, and Britain; and Chinese emigrants to Singapore, Taiwan, and Hong Kong."[6] While the United States has experienced increased rates of large body mass and obesity-related difficulties, predominantly diabetes, the most susceptible peoples are the Pacific Islanders (Native Hawaiians, Samoans, and Nauruans) who are experiencing greater problems. The "greatest impact of obesity-related disorders will continue to be in newly industrialized and developing nations like Asia, Africa, the Caribbean, Latin America, and the Indian and Pacific Oceans, which historically had an unstable food supply."[7] The explanation lies within the last comment: unstable food supply.

As is true for not only those listed above living in cultures not accustomed to plentiful and high-fat food, a similar problem is found in the United States among peoples who had a less-than-stable food supply before arriving in the United States: Mexicans and Africans. Their survival had been dependent upon developing a "thrifty gene" that allowed them to store fat for the lean times when food was not available. Upon arrival in the United States, even if they remained economically insecure, food access was not a problem. Yet, their physiologies, evolved to store fat efficiently, could not metabolize the plentiful and fatty food intake. They are genetically inclined to be overweight— and to become ill—once exposed to U.S. food and lifestyle.[8]

Usually not considered prone to being fat, Asian children and adults (Chinese, Japanese, Filipinos, and Malaysians) are becoming hard-hit by the sugary and fatty foods as introduced by U.S. fast food chains. Not unexpectedly, given our globalized standards of beauty, the ballooning of Asians has been met with the same response as in the United States: "a proliferation of gyms, slimming programs, diet pills, and liposuction."[9]

Even the French are eating more like Americans and, as a result, getting fatter. But it is all relative. While the French are sporting a slightly fuller figure, their obesity rate is about 10 percent, while the U.S. rate is triple that.[10]

As suggested, the main reason for this expansion of people's body sizes globally is the desire for profit. Paul Krugman hits the nail on the head when he writes, "Fat is a fiscal issue," meaning that there is money to be made in obesity.[11] Clearly, there is a great deal of money to be made selling fast food to Asians and exporting high-sugar, high-fat food to Micronesians. Better yet, from the profit motive point of view, we can manufacture food more cheaply using ingredients (like high fructose corn syrup and palm oil) that are not healthy for us to consume and that put on more weight than do traditional ingredients (like cane sugar and vegetable oil). In the early 1970s, food scientists developed a method by which to make a cheaper sweetener: high-fructose corn syrup (HFCS). It is made from corn rather than cane sugar and is six times sweeter. Importantly, the cost of producing this high-sugar product was markedly less than that of ordinary sugar. Moreover, HFCS ensures a long shelf-life in foods, so high-calorie junk food as found in vending machines can be kept fresh-tasting for a long time with no need to replace them frequently (thus saving money). Soda companies went from using a 50/50 blend of sugar and corn syrup to 100 percent HFCS because HFCS is remarkably cheaper. Unfortunately, HFCS is quite dysfunctional for the human metabolism, skewing the metabolism toward fat storage.[12] But health issues matter naught, as the concern at the United States Department of Agriculture was "pure farm economics."[13]

Palm oil (also known as "tree lard"), unlike vegetable oil, is chemically similar to beef tallow and is a highly saturated fat. It is also stunningly cheap to produce. Palm oil was transformed into a viable commercial fat in the 1970s, and its use is widespread in the manufacture of convenience and fast foods (French fries, pastries). As with HFCS, it has the added "advantage" of allowing products made with it to last a very long time thus ending the need to constantly replenish supermarket shelves. Not only is palm oil tastier than many vegetable oils (it is similar, molecularly, to lard), it is very inexpensive to make and use. Regardless of the downsides for our health and body size, price was the determinant in its use.[14]

Another good way to make a buck was to increase portion size. Portion sizes and "value marketing" became effective tools to increase sales and profits at fast food and other restaurants. Unsurprisingly, it was found that if people were offered large serving sizes at a good price, they would buy more. So portion sizes were increased and prices lowered, and food manufacturers made a killing. In a 20-year period (1970s—1990s), serving sizes expanded from two to five times larger than they had been before the 1970s.[15] It was roughly at that time (particularly in the 1980s) that fast food restaurants were having trouble making profits. Larger portions at lower prices saved the day.[16]

Perception is important in the food service industry. With increased portion sizes, calories were increased, as were the profits, without an increase in perception of gluttony. Buying two boxes of popcorn looked "piggish," but one huge box of popcorn was still just one box.[17] Likewise, McDonald's could get people to buy more fries by selling them in jumbo-sized bags, allowing consumers to not look like gluttons, since they weren't eating numerous bags. This was the origin of "supersizing."[18]

Where money is involved, we will find politico-economic influence and lobbying. In an article about the abysmal state of high school eating habits, the issue comes down to balanced diets versus balanced budgets. Coca-Cola, Pizza Hut, and other high-calorie fast food commercial interests are prevalent in the U.S. educational system. It is not necessarily that our school systems don't care about the health of our children and teenagers. But underfunded public schools whose budgets do not allow for needed educational resources, rely on profit-oriented corporations to supply the resources (such as textbooks) they need in exchange for contracts with soda and other convenience food companies selling unhealthy food to schoolchildren.[19] We now have a situation in which fast food makes up a substantial portion of total food sales, as is the case in 71 percent of California schools. In essence, because of budget cuts to education, school children have been eating high-calorie, poor quality food, and becoming heavy. Aside from the bribery of fast-food-supplied educational needs, school cafeteria meals have been outsourced. These assembled-elsewhere cafeteria meals are of unknown but suspiciously poor quality, much like TV dinners.[20] However, given the U.S. budgetary crisis, healthy food service in the school cafeteria, because it costs money, is not going to "make it onto the agenda."[21]

In response to being told that we should watch our diets, up sprang a lobbying group, which says uncategorically that we should not be intimidated by the "food police." In opposition to the Centers for Disease Control and other research institutes, the Center for Consumer Freedom discounts the obesity epidemic and the dangers of obesity. The Center for Consumer Freedom does make some good fat-acceptance and fat-and-fit points, such as I have noted in the looks and health chapter (Chapter 1). Their arguments are tainted, however, when we discover that the Consumer Freedom group is sponsored by food manufacturers. Corporate contributors who finance this group include Coca-Cola, Wendy's, Tyson Foods, and Outback Steakhouse.[22]

Capitalism, Size, and Beauty

There is indeed money to be made from obesity. In a nutshell, corporations will sell us the plus-size clothing as well as diet pills. Given that people-of-size comprise a majority (two-thirds by most estimates) of the U.S. population, one might say people-of-size are hardly a niche market. Businesses are responding to the demand for plus-size items including: larger towels, larger beds, larger clothes, larger clothes hangars, larger jewelry, larger furniture, larger coffins, seatbelt extenders, larger umbrellas, scales that can weigh up to 1,000 pounds, and plus-size-oriented workout videotapes. Medical-equipment manufacturers have supersized stretchers, with thicker aluminum frames, bulkier connectors and extra spine supports with a capacity of 650 pounds.[23] We have available bigger bedding, office chairs built with heavy-gauge steel and high-tension support for people weighing up to 500 pounds, automobiles with extra inches of elbow room in the interiors, extra-large coffins that can hold bodies up to 700 pounds.[24]

Another entrepreneurial venture is "size-friendly" resorts. Freedom Paradise, south of Cancun, Mexico, offers "large armless chairs, wide steps with railings in swimming pools, walk-in showers instead of bathtubs, stronger hammocks, and a staff steeped in sensitivity training." In sum, while some might argue that what is needed is a solution to obesity, we have instead entrepreneurs making money from obesity. At the same time, as an entrepreneur-of-size remarks, "The fact of the matter is that we're big, and we need the same things that thin people do."[25]

Some of this economic activity is direct, as in the examples I just gave. And some of this activity has a more indirect, spillover effect. As an illustration, let us consider diet programs. Durham, North Carolina is the diet capital of the world, the hometown of the Rice Diet Program, the Duke Diet and Fitness Center, and Structure House. These diet programs themselves are quite expensive, as witnessed by Jean Renfro Anspaugh who dieted at the Rice House.[26] But the diet programs are just a start for the money to be made. Dieters pump more than $51 million a year into the local Durham economy. The secondary spending, beyond the primary diet center fees, includes new sneakers (when their feet shrink), new eyeglasses (when their diabetes improves), and cosmetic surgery (when loose skin replaces the reduced heft). Skin-tucking plastic surgery alone can cost about $25,000 per person. Plus, the dieters pay rent, set up temporary workplaces, and purchase permanent housing.[27]

Clothes, of course, comprise a huge economic market and manufacturers do not want to miss out on the need for large-size clothing. Indeed, larger-size clothing is "one of the fastest growing segments in apparel right now," with children's plus-size market growing at a faster rate than adult plus-size clothes.[28] Young, plus-size shoppers are increasingly important to retailers, with plus-size apparel sales rising about 14 percent, compared to 5.6 percent for all women's clothes.[29] Clothing designers, marketers, and manufacturers have also begun to realize the desire for *attractive* and fashionable plus-size clothing, clothes that are not drab and intended to hide the body. We find a recent growing awareness among teenagers that they don't "have to be thin" and a "major backlash" has replaced the thin ideal with fat acceptance as viewed in teens-of-size clothing preferences. Girls, particularly, are taking pride in "normal" body shapes, by wearing tank tops, halter-tops, and other revealing clothing even though they're heavy. With fat acceptance, teens-of-size have a better self-image than used to be the case, and that would seem to be a good thing. But there remains a worried uncertainty among many about whether we should be rewarding fatness with acceptance, whether we should adopt generous attitudes toward generous-sized bodies. If we as a society make plus sizes acceptable, some think, we are encouraging poor health behaviors, such as not exercising and overeating.[30]

Whether we see this economic activity as commercial exploitation or as evidence of fat-acceptance, it is clear that capitalism's influence on how we respond to our appearance is not new and it is here to stay.

The capitalism-beauty nexus may be assisted by voluntary participation on the part of consumers rather than the result of solely intentional exploitation on the part of corporations. That is, we spend money to look good and we at least think we do so willingly. Nevertheless, the main point stands that a good deal of money is spent on improving our physical appearance to make ourselves socially desirable. As we have seen throughout this book, women are the more prominent targets of such angst to be beautiful (young, thin, etc.) but men are by no means immune to consumerism in the name of appearance improvement. Men are equally subject to capitalist pressures to look as good as they can, according to a study of *Men's Health* magazine advertisements; and today's male identity is based on consumption, a traditional role for women. According to the author of the analysis, "Branded masculinity is rooted in consumer capitalism wherein corporate profit can be enhanced by generating insecurity about one's body and one's consumer choices and then offering a solution through a particular corporate brand." *Men's Health* advertisements advise men, successfully, to not only gain muscles and buy fashionable clothes, but to also strive for "the appearance of financial success as the necessary characteristics for a real man today."[31] Relying on insecurity about their bodies coupled with the seductions of consumer capitalism, the advertisements instruct the men on what to wear and what to drive, as well as how to have a stylish hard body.[32] *Real men* "must today demonstrate their manliness through consumption of the *right* products."[33]

Social Class and Appearance

A myriad of physical traits can make or break us, socially, and the ability to pay for a good physical appearance is by no means equally distributed. Hair coloring and styling, expensive cosmetics, nice clothes, skin made clear and unblemished by dermatology and good health care, plastic surgery, and well-cared-for teeth are not available to all.

Socioeconomic status, the term sociologists use to describe social class, is comprised of three factors: income, education, and occupation. Socioeconomic status, or class, is affected by many variables such as race and ethnicity, gender, family background, age, and so on. For the most part, we have little control over our class; for instance, we cannot control who our parents are and thus the status we are born into. If our parents are poor, we are likely to be also. True, we can strive to improve our status by getting an education but getting an education is no guarantee of getting a good job with good pay. And getting an education is, for that matter, not guaranteed. Education costs money, a great deal of it. And education as well as the other avenues to improving one's station in life (marrying a person of greater status than oneself, for instance) is much influenced by one's physical appearance. People-of-size, for example, are more likely to experience much lower college admission rates and to be denied letters of recommendation (the kiss of death for college entrance and for jobs).[34]

As I have mentioned in an earlier chapter, poor people are more likely to be obese. Plus, there are financial consequences to being heavy, and these consequences are "not restricted to loss of employment opportunities and lower salaries. Being fat costs more."[35] People-of-size have to pay more for their clothes (check the clothing catalogs and you'll find that plus sizes are priced higher), for their health insurance, and for rental housing. On the other hand, thin people with chronic health problems such as birth defects, asthma, and diabetes "did not suffer economic and social consequences...despite their disabilities."[36]

Where we find double discrimination is in instances of bias against groups that are already oppressed: Mexican Americans, African Americans, women of any color, and poor people. People in these categories are more frequently heavy, and discriminated against for being so, compared to other groups. We know that racial and ethnic minorities are more likely to be unemployed and underemployed; add size issues and the under-and unemployment difficulties increase. And we know that women-of-size, compared to thin women, are more likely to lose or never gain socioeconomic status "regardless of their achievement test scores or family wealth." Women-of-size earn incomes far below thin women by about a three-to-one margin.[37]

A question that has been raised lately is whether being of a poorer social class leads to obesity or being of larger size leads to fewer socioeconomic opportunities (good jobs, higher education, and advantageous marriages) and thus being in a lower social class. The answer may be endemic to the environment, notably the lack of exercise facilities and opportunities available in inner cities and poor rural areas. In the 1980s, our public schools experienced a scarcity of financial resources, ridding the schools of gym classes and other financial support for physical education and athletic programs. Fitness opportunities "for children grew increasingly class-based. In the nation's more affluent suburbs [there were] sports clubs for children."[38] Children's fitness activities grew increasingly dependent upon class, via parental time and money, bearing in mind that poorer parents lack money and possibly lack time if they are working more than one job as is increasingly the case. And, as we are well aware, recreational spending is greater in the suburbs than in blighted urban areas or in poorer rural areas, allowing the "burbs" to offer parks and other safe environs in which to walk or jog, a commodity absent in less well-endowed areas.[39] Not surprisingly then, the working and poorer classes, proportionately overrepresented by nonwhites, exercise far less than the more affluent and white and they watch a lot of TV instead.[40]

While the better-off may have access to looks-improving goods and services (dental care, hair care, skin care, exercise programs, etc.), they may, interestingly, need such goods and services less than the working class and the poor. Virginia Blum observes that, "the socially privileged need not concern themselves as much in general with their physical appearance. While they may be the ones for whom cosmetic interventions are most affordable, they are also the least in need of the image building and sustaining supplied by making an attractive appearance in the world. The socially privileged have advantages that shield their self-esteem from the rude and inquisitive opprobrium of strangers." In other words, when one is not well-heeled, physical appearance counts a lot more. Without the advantages of club membership, name-dropping, and other class-related benefits, making a good impression is absolutely essential. Our fates can be sealed for better or worse by our physical appearance, if we are not financially well-endowed. We can gain social privilege by our good looks, while social privilege already possessed is not reliant upon our looks.[41]

Appearance as Commodity

Naomi Wolf (1991) describes beauty as "not a universal or natural category but rather a form of cultural 'currency' used by male institutions to limit and control women's access to power. Within this economy, beauty is not merely a desirable asset but a 'legitimate and necessary qualification' for a woman's rise in power."[42] Professional success is dependent upon this "capital" and so women (and increasingly men) strive to stay as ageless as possible, to dress and groom ourselves appropriately, to be as beautiful as we can be. A new beauty-based "meritocracy" has overtaken women's skills, education, talents, and capabilities. The really bad news is that such a "meritocracy" ensures and justifies women's secondary status in the workplace. So, while greater beauty may result in upward mobility (better jobs, better pay) in some fashion, it also keeps us in our place as objects to be evaluated on our looks rather than on our abilities. Another significant reminder put forward by Wolf is the amount of time and energy women spend on trying to be beautiful. This investment in beautification necessarily prohibits women's investment on the much more salient tasks in life such as advancing our political and economic power.[43]

Similarly, Nancy Etcoff reports that more money is "spent on beauty than on education or social services" in the United States.[44] This is an intriguing fact, upon examination, because it not only suggests the vacuousness of our society (that we would focus on such superficial behaviors as beautifying ourselves), but also explains why we continue to engage in such pointless pursuits. That is, if we're not educated, we may rely on our looks to get ahead. Keep this thought in mind for the next and final chapter in which I suggest that education, as a form of awareness raising, would be helpful in gaining a more personally and socially functional grip on beauty-based inequality.

CHAPTER 10

Conclusion: Toward an Acceptance of Looks Diversity

In this book, we have learned that achieving or failing to meet beauty standards can determine our economic and social lives. I have summarized how this happens, as when appearance affects romance and family, workplace experience, and health care. I have described the industries (cosmetics and cosmeceuticals, diet, fitness, supplements, and plastic surgery) that have developed in response to our dissatisfaction with our looks, while at the same time *encouraging* our dissatisfaction. I have discussed the manner in which the medical and insurance professions, the legal community, and the economy influence how we feel about our appearance, as when we are denied health care and airplane seating, when we must rely on civil suits to guarantee employment, and when we are unfavorably compared to a globalized ideal of beauty—because of what we look like.

We know that even the most minute and simplest defining characteristics (height, "beauty," nose shape, tooth color, skin color, hair texture, eye shape, etc.) are important markers upon which we are judged. These traits can be subject to disagreement; at the same time, there is a great deal of universality in beauty standards especially as the world becomes a global community. We know that our looks are largely beyond our control; for instance, we all age and we are all born as a particular race. We know that public reaction to physical appearance is greatly determined by media, capitalism, advertising, and so forth.

Yet there is much more to learn, not only about these appearance-based social processes mentioned here, but also about the similarities of looks bias to other forms of social bias such as sexism, racism, classism, ableism, and ageism. Societal response to our physical appearance, particularly when it results in discrimination, is a rights issue in itself; and appearance as a rights issue overlaps with other minority rights issues as visited upon, say, heavy women and not-young women. At the beginning and at the end of this study, I find that physical appearance ought not be, but is terribly, relevant to our place in life.

At this final juncture, let us consider whether we, as a society or more broadly as a global community, can expect greater acceptance of a wide range of physical appearances. After laying out the indicators of progress and the methods by which looks-diversity-acceptance may come about (social movements, media attention, education, and interpersonal interaction), I bring forward a couple of new ideas about (what I call) opposite or unexpected bias, having to do with the disadvantages of beauty and the notion of plus-size superiority. This opposite or unexpected bias, as opposed to the usual bias, such as I have described throughout this book, also points to inequality. My main message here is that inequality and bias are never functional no matter at whom they are aimed. I further propose that the freedom to choose, to change or not change our looks, is key. Finally, if appearance-inequality is an individual as well as a social problem for whole cultures, discourse about it will expose its existence and will generate awareness. Thus, solutions appear.

Progress, Regress, and Stasis

To synopsize, we have a mixture of good and less good news, with a miniscule, slow-growing acceptance of diverse physical traits (size, age, skin color, etc.). As I'll briefly discuss in the next section, some of these advances have come about from legal action and policy change, while probably more have come about via grassroots awareness raising. The acceptance of looks-diversity, such as it is in its nascent form, follows the similar, historical growth pattern of other diversity acceptance as we have seen with civil rights, sexual orientation rights, disability rights, and so on. Forces for change, be they formal (legal and policy changes) or more informal (awareness raising), escalate each other. With formal changes come greater awareness of the issues of inequality (such as lack of physical access, employment discrimination, and so on), while informal changes rely upon and propel forward the more formalized changes.

Progress

In a small way, women and girls are rejecting media and other pressures to look a certain way. Today, a growing number of them believe they possess the freedom to dress how they want, gain or lose weight, wear make-up or not, and so on "without fear that their value as a woman or their seriousness as a person is at stake."[1]

Accepting a variety of body sizes would indicate progress, if by "progress" we mean social acceptance. What may appear to be progress and acceptance is elusive and complicated, however. To specify, what appears to be progress may not really be or may be merely the dangerous *appearance* of progress. The use of plus-size mannequins in our department stores looks like progress until we learn that the "plus-size" mannequins are size 8–16 with the size 8 having hip measurements of 38 inches. Campaigns for "real beauty" put forward by the Dove cosmetics company are diluted when we realize that the models in the Dove ads, representing "larger" women, are size 6–14, who, in reality, are small to average.[2] Another way to put it is to ask, referring to the Dove models, "Are the women in the company's new ad campaign too big to sell beauty products, or have our minds gotten too small?"[3] More pointedly, the Dove ads

> challenge society's beauty ideals. But they are also designed to sell beauty products. In the end, they may make us more obsessed with our looks. First, the "real women" are hardly that. The average American woman is 5′4″ and weighs 150 pounds, meaning that half of all women are larger. Real women have curves, but they also have scars, lumps, stretch marks and big patches of cellulite—noticeably absent from the women in the ads. Seeing so-called real models who are still slimmer, younger and firmer than many real-real women is even more disheartening than looking at stick-thin ones. We know that the waifs are unreal. But to find that you're bigger than a "plus-size" model—how depressing is that? Setting a slightly larger physical standard is not much better than an ultra-thin one.[4]

Indeed, size zero is not small enough. The prevailing message has been that we must starve ourselves until, literally, we collapse and die as one did after her turn at the fashion catwalk. Luckily, there has been quite a backlash, cross-culturally, recently against the use of "too-thin" fashion models.[5] Spain, India, Great Britain, Italy, and the United States have joined a chorus of concern about frail, famished bodies used as models for what we should strive to be.

While the new mannequins and cosmetic ads have their restrictive sides, notably using models who are not representative of average imperfect human specimens, another viewpoint is that the use of larger mannequins and beyond size-zero models is a step in the right direction. Bodily heaviness, if it is becoming more acceptable, is so because it is normal, common, and average. This has been shown to be the case for children, with declining stigma coinciding with the increasing childhood obesity rate. An account of childhood obesity finds, "With so many children and parents being overweight and obese, there's little stigma attached to being fat."[6] Likewise, heavy adults, surveyed about their attitudes toward their own size, say they are not disturbed by their size because are surrounded by so many heavy people. In other words, and as reported in a recent nationwide fitness survey of overweight people, the majority of people in the United States are overweight, so being overweight is not considered problematic but is considered average and normal. An alternative explanation is that, cognitively, the overweight may self-protectively see their weight as non-problematic more than would their thinner counterparts. Nevertheless, the overweight and sedentary, as discovered in this report, view their size and inactivity as the accepted norm and they are correct at least in the numerical sense.[7] In support, behavioral measures show that we eat more and we eat more high-fat food, while worrying less about our weight.[8] Not all agree that this is a sign of progress out of concern for health issues. Strictly speaking from a size-acceptance point of view, however, it is a form of normalization.

U.S. attitudes, on the part of all-sized people, though not unequivocal, have shifted from rejection toward acceptance of heavy people. Over a 20-year-period, surveyed Americans say they are now less likely to find overweight people unattractive: currently 24 percent of the respondents say that heavy people are not less attractive because of their weight, compared to a previous 55 percent who said so. In sum, there have been attitude shifts not only toward greater acceptance but also toward *liking* larger sizes. A counterargument to this conclusion is that the public is growing more politically correct and does not want to display bias against people-of-size.[9]

An important sign that our society has normalized larger-sized bodies is the plethora of large-sized products and services available, as noted in the chapter on the economy (Chapter 9). The availability of stylish clothing in plus sizes, always having been available to smaller-sized people, alleviates some of the social strain of being heavy and being stigmatized for being so. Yes, this clothing costs more and is not so easy to find (sometimes "hidden" on online sites and in the recesses of department stores) but such clothing is increasingly purchasable and increasingly front-and-center.[10]

Another way to look at acceptance and normalization is to consider the opposite of it, the *rejection* of beauty standards. The Miss America beauty contest, once a big draw on national TV, has been dropped by ABC television. An ABC senior program executive observed, "It simply was not performing for us. We've lost money on it." TV ratings for the pageant have been in free fall for over 10 years. Viewership dropped by 15 million, from 25 million viewers in 1995 to less than 10 million in 2004, despite limiting the talent contest and adding skimpier swimsuits.[11] One explanation is that TV shows featuring scantily clad beautiful women, such as *Desperate Housewives*, are plentiful and have made beauty pageants less of a novelty. In other words, beauty is common and so is nakedness.[12]

Regress

On the lack of progress, Naomi Wolf writes, "the latest fashions for seven- and eight-year-olds re-create the outfits of pop stars who dress like sex workers," clearly a sign of continuing objectification.[13] Media outlets display very young, beautiful girls (sometimes children) representing what adult women should look like and what men of all ages should want.

The homogenization of beauty standards via globalization and cookie-cutter plastic surgery, described in this book, is not a sign of progress but rather a sign of probable regress to a tightened, restricted set of appearance criteria. To illustrate the reduced variety in beauty standards, we find that African American models have Anglo features and lighter-toned skin, while white models are selected for thick lips or have surgical implants to thicken their lips.[14] In other words, we "smooth out all racial, ethnic, and sexual 'differences' that disturb Anglo-Saxon, heterosexual expectations and identifications."[15]

The many innovations in the quest to make ourselves as appearance-acceptable as possible, from cosmetic treatments to diets to plastic surgery and even genetic design, are signs of technological progress, while they are simultaneously signs of a continuing rejection of naturalness and variation. Moreover, all appearance alterations have very much to do with money, which excludes a great number of us who cannot afford such engineering.

The very term "designer babies" connotes wealth, according to a eugenics expert. Depending upon the family's financial circumstances, features such as eye color, height, and weight can become elective. A sperm bank on the west coast "caters exclusively to Americans who desire Scandinavian sperm from select and screened Nordics," with the options for appearance choices being endless.[16] Apart from the financially undemocratic nature of genetic design, one might ask if such engineering is a bad or a good thing for society. James Watson, the codiscoverer of the double helix and celebrated geneticist, declared in 2003: "People say it would be terrible if we made all girls pretty. I think it would be great." He neglected to say why it would be "great" to be surrounded only by pretty girls.[17] Nor did he address the downsides of a monoculture of pretty girls. If pretty girls are plentiful or all we have, the standards for "pretty" would likely become narrower and more unreachable.

Also on the continuing rejection of looks-diversity, and in counter-argument to my above recitation of size-acceptance, we have continuing resistance to accepting and normalizing larger-sized bodies. Societal accommodations to larger-sized people (larger restaurant seating, plus-sized clothing, etc.) is not a positive move, according to some, since these accommodations come with "a price, and perhaps a sizeable one."[18] Mostly, critics of the fat-acceptance movement state their case in terms of concerns about the health consequences of obesity, firmly believing that, contrary to the healthy-at-any-size argument, heaviness is not healthy. Not always separate from the health issue is the revulsion that some feel about a world without right-and-wrong, good-and-bad boundaries. Greg Critser, for example, writes that the fat-acceptance movement has taken place in "the wishful-thinking, reality-denying, boundary-hating world of modern America."[19] We *must*, in this view, adhere to parameters of acceptable appearance; to do otherwise is a violation of or a negation of those strictures. Tautological reasoning, to be sure.

The dangerous other side to the coin is the continuing proliferation of anorexia and bulimia. Children as young as 7 years old as well as older (middle-aged) people suffer from eating disorders, with bulimia nervosa (binge-eating and forced vomiting) being two to five times more common than anorexia nervosa (a severely restricted food intake). Moreover, anorexics and bulimics learn the methods of these eating disorders from tips provided by online Internet chatrooms. Much has become widely known about this often-fatal behavior, as witnessed by the multitude of books and other materials on the subject, yet presently there are pro-anorexia Web sites encouraging it.[20]

Stasis

On the homeostasis side, it is noteworthy that once we bound the feet of young Chinese girls to make them more desirable in the marriage market, and now we have foot beautification surgery. Women have shed their corsets of yesterday, but now we undergo the discomfort of bikini waxing.[21] And, sure, we can buy plus-size clothing. We are simultaneously encouraged to buy diet pills. So, while there are indices of a move toward looks-acceptance and away from rigid beauty standards, there are at least as many indices suggesting that little has changed.

Movement toward Equality: How to Change the Picture

In large part, but with caveats, the media, the advertisers, and the manufacturers of cosmetics, clothing, and pharmaceuticals have inhibited looks equality by substantiating our biases, toward ourselves and toward others. We are socialized to try to be as beautiful as possible through diets, diet pills, cosmetic use, surgery, and so on, and mostly we fail to reach the supermodel pinnacle, culminating in self-blame of considerable proportions. The hard evidence of social bias (job and other discrimination) subsequently reinforces the industry-imposed biases. Charged with combating these well-entrenched biases are egalitarian movements, advocacy, and activism.

I have suggested that greater acceptance of looks-diversity will follow a similar path that societies have experienced regarding racism, sexism, ableism, and ageism. However, looks-bias is a much tougher issue in several ways. For one thing, appearance *overlaps* with race, gender, age, etc., and these overlaps speak to double discrimination, as we have seen when Asian eyes are not considered so appealing as round eyes, black skin reaps fewer rewards than white skin, older faces are turned away from jobs that are given to those with younger faces. Another distinction between looks biases and other biases is, as noted throughout this book, we *blame* people for their looks, maligning people for what they look like, as though it is their personal fault. Racism, sexism, and other ism's are more difficult to defend than looks-ism because race, gender, age, and disability are, for one, clearly beyond one's control and, for another, are no longer "politically correct" to express openly. These ism's are also illegal when expressed as discrimination.[22] So far, it remains largely legal to discriminate on looks.

Awareness is the key to social change. Awareness comes about through the activities of social movements, the media, education, and interpersonal interaction. These activities lay the groundwork for policy changes and legislation, which, in turn, formalize and solidify the legitimacy of the movement.

Social Movements

The fat-acceptance movement began in the early 1970s, with the Fat Underground being established in 1973 as a more radical alternative to the National Association to Advance Fat Acceptance (NAAFA).[23] The fat-acceptance movement, peopled mostly by women and with its feminist overtones, has something of a problem since, as Marilyn Wann points out, the absence of fat men participating in the movement means that size-acceptance has less clout. She clarifies, "as long as people think of fat as a women's issue and a question of vanity, they will continue to disregard the seriousness of antifat prejudice."[24]

Essentially, size-acceptance movements, as is true for all equal rights movements, hope to promote acceptance and fight discrimination by means of advocacy and by visible, lawful actions to bring public attention to the fact that *differences* do not mean inferiority and that equal rights ought to be available for all regardless of size. Mostly, size-acceptance movements refer to width or girth. Importantly, there are a few other organizations that educate the public about other forms of size-ism and advocate for equality; for instance, the International Size Acceptance Association's Great Heights group is a tallness-based focus group, the ISAA Aspirations group refers to a shortness-based focus group, and the ISAA Natural Tendencies group is a naturally thin-based focus group. By far, however, the most successful and most publicly visible size-acceptance groups are the fat-acceptance organizations.[25]

Apart from size-acceptance movements, there is, regretfully, no known social movement advancing equality for the socially deemed unattractive, the disfigured, and the plain. There are auxiliary movements that relate to physical appearance such as movements demanding equal rights for the disabled and the aged (notably, the Gray Panthers), but there are no such movements for the ordinarily unattractive.

While "ugly laws", mentioned in the Preface and in the Introduction, no longer exist, it is startling that formalized exclusion and punishment of the "unsightly" (disabled, maimed, deformed, and the diseased) was once codified by law. These "ugly laws," also known as "unsightly beggar" laws, were similar to vagrancy laws forbidding certain people (namely the poor) from venturing forth in public, except with the added offense of being unsightly. Unsightly beggars, during the time of these ordinances, could be fined and imprisoned for being seen in public places. The last of these laws, Chicago municipal code 36-34, was repealed in 1974, yet the effects linger on in a more informal and covert way. As Susan Schweik has pointed out, the laws are gone as evidence of blatant looks-prejudice but more subtle and equally lethal are the noncodified norms permitting social exclusion. Speaking of facial disfigurements, for example, she writes that "legalized discrimination against capable people with facial anomalies in our postugly era is still remarkably widespread" and concludes that the "quieter forms of scapegoating work more efficiently."[26] No formalized social movement rid our society of ugly laws, although there were smatterings of public protest against them. They were rendered unusable by virtue of being unenforceable.

Media Influence

One method of promoting acceptance is media attention to the topic and, more subtly, the use of a variety of people (race-wise, age-wise, looks-wise, etc.) in media outlets (television shows, movies, advertisements, newspapers, magazines, and music). The media thus far have a very poor record of primarily using only attractive people in their broadcasts (including news shows), movies, advertisements, and so on. The media have also imbedded stereotypes by not casting heavy women in a positive light (for instance, as romantic interests) and, on the rare occasions when the disabled are shown, casting them as asexual. More recently, the media have been, albeit in small increments, responsible for size awareness taking hold, with TV shows and live plays using size themes and using actors-of-size.[27] We have quite a way to go yet, as we read in the chapter on workplace about the renowned and greatly talented opera singer Deborah Voigt being fired from her job for being too big, as though her weight has anything to do with her singing ability. She did the job-saving thing: she had a gastric by-pass. The bypass was the personally wise thing to do, since it saved her career. Unfortunately, the bypass and her resulting weight loss then disallowed audiences from seeing that a heavy woman can do the job as well as a thinner one, thus reaffirming that (a) heavy people are not as capable as thinner people and (b) it is socially and legally okay to discriminate against people based on their appearance. As a further illustration of the public and the entertainment industry not getting it quite right, a recent play entitled

Fat Pig about a woman-of-size being rejected by a man because of her size triggered no howl of dissent. Although the man truly liked her, her size was an embarrassment to him. This play and its message were publicly accepted as a viable story.[28] In sum the media could do more to promote looks diversity and awareness.

Educational Influences

Education is key to diversity-acceptance, and looks-acceptance would be no exception. Education is a formalized teaching and learning process, offering as-near-to-the-truth-as-we-know-it information on an array of topics. In the case of biases, education has played a significant role in (a) bringing a multitude of diverse races, nationalities, sexual orientations, etc. together in classrooms, (b) describing examples of previous and current forms of bias (for example, the anti-Semitism of Nazi Germany, women's struggles for voting rights and equal pay, white supremacy in the United States, etc.) as well as responses to those biases (rights movements, etc.), and (c) offering mountainous research findings on the nature of bias. While we have few college courses on looks-acceptance, social scientists are beginning to provide conference sessions on the topic and a number of textbooks are now available.[29] It has been said that bias is ignorance, thus education is the solution to bias.[30]

Interpersonal Influences

Although we usually don't think about informal interpersonal communication as having an effect on public awareness, consciousness-raising does come about, and very significantly so, through individual-level, interpersonal interaction. We saw this happen historically with other biases such that, now, it is unusual for polite society to emit racist or sexist remarks. We have policed ourselves, over time, to not let racist and sexist comments slide. When people make biased remarks about the less-then-beautiful ("Good grief, she's fat!" "What awful teeth! Why doesn't he get them fixed?" "Hey, shorty!"), it would be awareness raising to not let it pass. To say nothing, as would be true with other biased remarks ("Women just can't do the job that a man can do," etc.) reinforces the prejudice. Instead, we can calmly and effectively disagree with such judgments. We can offer alternative ways of looking at the plain, the large, the short, the less-than-beautiful as equals ("Well, her size doesn't hinder her job as a teacher/engineer/police officer/etc." "He may not be able to afford dental care." "And?"). A useful and noninsulting strategy is to briefly present the conditions that make for less-than-beautiful features, such as economic explanations for physical features. Another is to point out the averageness of some of these features. Once we have the listener's attention, we might overview the advantages and disadvantages faced by all of us, depending upon our appearance, regarding job experiences, romantic prospects, and other life circumstances. Chances are the critics have had similar experiences; after all, most of us are not beautiful, including those who judge others on their looks. Faced with a nonagreement response, critics do reconsider their biases. It is as though they really hadn't thought of looks-bias before. Most people haven't.

Legislative and Policy Changes

Beyond the purely social-network biases (such as exclusion from friendships, marriage, and club memberships), which are difficult to document and not usually subject to legal action, legislation is the remedy to the more concrete forms of discrimination such as obstacles to physical access, employment, housing, and educational opportunities. As we have learned here, litigation against size discrimination is slowly becoming part of social reality.[31] While there have been inroads in size equality, policy-wise and legislatively, we have also seen with the NAAFA's Fat Feminist Caucus that such successes are not easily transferred to the broader culture.[32] Yet our society is farther ahead than we would have been without these policy changes.

Unexpected Biases: What We Can Learn from the Reverse Picture

It is always helpful to turn research questions inside out, having investigated them from all other angles. This study has mostly been about the social advantages commensurate with features considered attractive, as socially defined. Let us briefly address the biases that those with "advantaged" looks encounter, not only in terms of "beauty" but also in terms of size as when thin people are viewed as inferior. These opposite or unexpected biases retain the hierarchy-inducing trait of the already discussed looks-based biases: denigration of one group as inferior by a "superior" group.

Pity for the Pretty?

Beauty can backfire, as noted in Chapter 3 on workplace. On the whole, let us consider whether people can be thought incapable or less capable because they are attractive. A very pretty female jockey faces two forms of discrimination, she says (and other jockeys say), because of her gender and her beauty. She claims to be denied ridership in the upper tiers of riders, such as the Triple Crown races, not because of her talent level but because of her looks. She is evaluated as "too pretty to be a jockey" and the male trainers "notice her looks before her talent or fail to take her seriously because of her feminine qualities."[33]

An educated, skilled, trained, and experienced librarian was turned down for promotion at Harvard University, she says, because of her looks. She has claimed in a lawsuit "that she has been rejected repeatedly for promotion because she is perceived as just a 'pretty girl' whose attire was too 'sexy.'" She was told that she would never be promoted at Harvard because, as her supervisor told her, she was a "joke" and was "seen merely as a pretty girl who wore sexy outfits, low-cut blouses, and tight pants."[34] She *could* alter her style of dress, but the question immediately leaps to mind, *should* she?

It's a little difficult to feel sorry for attractive people since they enjoy enormous social advantages and privileges. Yet, there may be curse-like fragments incurred from being beautiful or handsome. Jock-like men, men with well-sculpted bodies, may be presumed to be not-so-smart. Beautiful women, especially if they are blonde, as witnessed by a myriad of blonde jokes, are assumed to be unendowed with mental acuity. One might speculate that attractive people are, indeed, not so capable as more ordinary-looking people because they have never had to be. Like the wealth-privileged, folklore surrounding attractive people may suggest that, because of their looks-advantages, they have not had to study, work hard, acquire skills, or even be nice. There is no foundation for this speculation, however, and it may very well be that attractive people work and study as hard as plain people.

All else being equal, attractive people unquestionably fare much better in life opportunities than do unattractive people, as this book and many others have shown. But a basic truth remains that looks are an artifice, an artificial marker for how people are viewed in terms of their talents, capabilities, personality, intelligence, and so on. To err on the side of social equality, it is better to suppose that attractive people are no more and no less capable than unattractive ones.

The Superior State of Heaviness

A related point that merits consideration is the notion of superiority attached to usually considered disadvantageous features, notably large body size, as put forward by a minority of fat-acceptance representatives. Various fat-acceptance organizations have argued that "fat is or should be beautiful."[35] This implies that we as whole societies should not just accept heaviness but revere it as "beautiful." Perhaps the word "beautiful" is being used for its eye-catching appeal and should not be taken too seriously or too literally. Be reminded, for example, that "Black is beautiful," a common saying in the 1960s and 1970s, did not presuppose that all Blacks are truly physically beautiful. As the race movement progressed, its supporters regardless of color, began to realize and to state that races are equal and none are superior. But back to the matter of size, it might be proposed, in the same way that thinness should not be revered, nor should heaviness.

Nonetheless, members of an NAAFA chapter paired heaviness to adjectives such as "'majestic,' 'powerful,' 'complete,' 'sensual,' and 'feminine.' The fat woman is . . . 'sassy, impertinent, disobedient.'"[36] These same traits can also apply to thin and medium-sized women, and are not unique to heavy women. Marilyn Wann points out the advantages of being fat without stating categorically that thin people are inferior. For example, heavy women are sexier since they possess greater estrogen levels than thin women, heavy people don't show wrinkles as much as thin people, heavy people don't get osteoporosis as might thin people, and so on.[37] Lara Frater's book *Fat Chicks Rule* usefully advises heavy people where to purchase clothes, what to do about physical access problems, where to locate sites for size-advocacy groups, how to deal with rude remarks, how to meet people, etc. Regretfully, Frater implies that thin people are stupid when she refers to "stupid skinny people." She also assumes that thin people throw up to stay thin, judging from a joke she repeats, and makes other antithin comments.[38] She encourages heavy people to say to themselves, "I am fat, I am beautiful," when it isn't necessarily true that fat or thin people are beautiful.[39] Lastly, consider the book title: *Fat Chicks Rule*. Why must they *rule*? In the interest of social equality, no particular size would rule. Body size can best be seen as an *equal* state of being, with no size (heavy, thin, or in-between) a *superior* state of being.

Size bias and all other appearance-biases are destructive of equal rights for all people, regardless of appearance. To that end, it would serve us well as individuals and as societies to concentrate on equality, not superiority, and to not promote an advantaged status of any particular category of people.

Viewing some categories of people as more deserving than others runs the risk of playing into the hands of political counterarguments against equal rights. The political right's argument has been that gays, women, racial minorities, the disabled, and disadvantaged others are given unfair advantages due to reverse discrimination. Referring to disadvantaged classes as "protected classes" ignores whole histories of intense discrimination and belittles the very real and valid notion of equal treatment. To argue that any category of people are inferior—be they attractive or plain— does nothing to remove bias and support equality.

Conclusion

Coleen Rowley, the former Federal Bureau of Investigation employee who blew the whistle on the Bureau for failing to investigate the terrorism suspect Zacarias Moussaoui (allegedly in training to take part in the events of September 11, 2001), ran for Congress in 2006. When Ms. Rowley retired from the FBI in 2004, she asked acquaintances for input about whether she should run for political office. Ms. Rowley does not style her hair, does not use cosmetics, wears eyeglasses, and in general does little to "fix up." She was advised to get a "makeover" if she wanted to make a successful run. She responded, "I've butted heads with a few people— anyone who tells me I have to spruce up my hair and buy a new wardrobe. I haven't worn make-up since I was 21. You have to be authentic and genuine in serving the populace."[40] She is no doubt aware that the public judges us by our looks and is probably aware that her chances of winning a seat as a Representative would have been greatly enhanced if she were to fix up. But should she? Of course she should be evaluated only for her abilities, her skills, her work experience, but will there be a time when people will be so considered?

Maybe. It is not close at hand but it would seem that the general social trend, apart from occasional setbacks, is in the direction of equality, mostly as we have seen in other rights movements (civil rights, women's rights, disabled rights, and so forth). As long as women acquiesced to dictates to behave as powerless, as physically weak, as not as smart as men, they could not expect to make headway as social and economic equals. As long as African Americans took a back seat, literally and figuratively, they would not be treated as equals. We will not be able to force, nor should we force, changes in personal preferences for particular physical features. If someone doesn't want to date or marry another person because of her or his looks, that's an unavoidable and perhaps unchangeable matter of personal opinion. However, if an employer or a college or an airline refuses to hire, admit, or allow access because of a person's looks, that is a violation of equal rights. It is our choice then to confront this bias and request equal treatment.

On a more personal and individual level, we can refuse to try to be younger than we are, more perfectly beautiful than we are, whiter than we are, taller than our genetics had in mind, etc. Besides creating a larger proportion of people with varietal appearance, I'm not sure that this refusal would accomplish a move toward equality. Nor would such a refusal to participate in the looks-race be the most self-serving route to take given the competition that we all face in seeking the social opportunities (jobs and the like) that we require to live successfully. Nonetheless, *choice* is integral. We should be free to choose to change our appearance or not. We needn't obey the commands of the multibillion-dollar advertising industry but we can if we want to.[41] If we want to work out, wear make-up, have surgery, and otherwise change our looks, we should feel free to do that (or not).

True, the pressure to expend enormous amounts of time and money, to undergo painful and dangerous procedures, to be more physically acceptable is a part of the sexism, ageism, racism, and the artificiality of "beauty." These pressures channel us into supporting industries that profit hugely from our willingness to be pitted against each other in a social-economic system that discriminates against us based on our physical attributes. More to the point, it would be socially beneficial to see ourselves and others in the nonvisible terms of capabilities and goodness.

If we could view this process in nonpersonal terms, as disinterested bystanders, we could see the futility of an eternally unfair looks race. If we recognize the biases for what they are—methods of exclusion—we will judge not. It starts with us.

Appendix A: Filmography

Fat Girl. A French film (2001), the story focuses on two sisters, the younger of whom is heavy. Essentially, the plot centers on the older and thinner of the two sisters hoping to lose her virginity at a vacation resort, but the story could just as easily have been told with any sized teenage girls (both heavy, neither heavy), since the fatness of the one sister had almost nothing to do with the basic story line. True, her size is brought up as a means of the thin sister making fun of her (as sisters will do), and there are some displays of her eating habits and desire for revealing clothes (for instance, short dresses) against her mother's suggestions. But almost entirely, the movie has nothing to do with size. Interestingly, the movie title, translated from French, is actually *For My Sister.* This alteration in title begs the question of why, for the U.S. audience, the title was changed to *Fat Girl.* I can only suppose the explanation lies in making the film more enticing.

Hairspray. A John Waters (1988) movie, starring two heavy people (Ricky Lake and Devine), *Hairspray* shows how a heavy high school teenaged girl can win local fame over a beautiful and thin girl. Lake and Divine (daughter and mother) shop for clothes at the marvelously named "Hefty Hideaway." Lake wins out over the much more attractive schoolmate via her dancing talent and personality. She even steals the good-looking girl's boyfriend. This is an unrealistic perhaps, but very refreshing film.

Muriel's Wedding. A 1994 Australian production, this film stars Toni Collette as a young, heavy woman who wants desperately to get married.

She does get married to a handsome swim champion who marries her in order to gain citizenship. She leaves him, deciding she's better off without him. Disconcertingly, the photo on the front of the film container is not of Toni Collette but instead is a photo of a thin woman in a wedding dress, being showered with confetti.

Real Women Have Curves. This film (2002), set in East Los Angeles, is about a Mexican American, heavy, young woman defying her mother's wishes to lose weight and to get married. Ana, played by America Ferrera, eats what she wants and desires to (and does) attend university. There are marvelous scenes of rebellion; one in particular is a scene in the sweatshop dress factory where Ana works part-time, alongside her sister, mother, and other heavy women. In this scene, the women (with the exception of Ana's mother) seem to bond over their size, via humor.

Shrek 2. The animated 2004 Shrek movie picks up where *Shrek* left off. In the first movie, Shrek, a fairy tale ogre, meets a beautiful princess, Fiona, who is beautiful only in the daytime. At night, she becomes ogre-ish herself with green skin, trumpet-like ears, a flat and blubbery face, a flat nose, and a fat body. Shrek sees her in the nighttime and loves her anyway, impressing her greatly that she is not loved only when she's beautiful. They fall in love and are partners. In the second movie, Shrek and Fiona lay hands on a secret formula that would allow her and him to be beautiful all the time. They decide not to go that route and remain as their ogre selves.

Super Size Me. This 2004 film is narrated by, directed by, and stars Morgan Spurlock. It is basically an invective against McDonald's restaurants. Starting out as a medium-sized, healthy man, Spurlock eats McD's meals three times a day for a month, the result being a deterioration of his health and an increase in his size: he gains weight and many of the markers of good health (liver, blood pressure, etc.) are negatively affected. Among his messages are the profit motive and capitalist incentives of the McDonald's corporation, harm to school children (poor lunch programs and no athletic programs), as well as the harm that comes to adults by eating high-fat diets.

Appendix B: Selected Resources

Size Acceptance Organizations

Dwarfism.org: Reaching New Heights, a site providing links to medical resources, specialized shopping needs, legal information, and political correctness issues. http://dwarfism.org.

International Size Acceptance Association (ISAA). http://size-acceptance. org.

Largesse: The Network for Size Esteem, a site offering size-diverse materials such as videos and printed matter as well as links to size-acceptance activities. http://eskimo.com/~Elargesse.

Little People of America, largely an advocacy and awareness group. http://lpaonline.org or http://littlepeopleofamerica.org.

The National Association to Advance Fat Acceptance (NAAFA). http://naafa.org

National Organization of Lesbians of Size (NOLOSE) is an advocacy organization for lesbians-, bisexual, and transgender women of size. http://nolose.org.

SeaFATtle, is a feminist size acceptance activist group. http://seaFATtle.

Tall Clubs International, an organization that promotes tall awareness and provides social activities for tall people. http://tall.org.

Legal Assistance for Discrimination Cases

Beyond Bias Diversity Training. http://beyondbias.org.
Council on Size and Weight Discrimination. http://cswd.org.
Persons with Disability Law Center. http://naafa.org/documents/
brochures/lawcenter.
United States Equal Employment Opportunity Commission. http://eeoc.
gov.

Cosmetic Surgery Sites

http://seattledocs.com.
http://uwcosmeticsurgery.org
http://yestheyrefake.net.

Cosmetic Site

http://campaignforrealbeauty.com.

Discussion Groups

Abundance Magazine offers online discussion as well as size-diverse art and
literature. http://abundancemagazine.com. See also http://ssbbwoman.
com.
Adios Barbie is an online size-acceptance journal. http://adiosbarbie.com.
BBW magazine offers fashion advice for women-of-size as well as articles
on romance and beauty tips. http://bbw.magazine.com. See also the
Grand Woman Web site at http://grandwoman.com.
Dimensions provides a site for women-of-size and fat admirers, and ad-
dresses sexuality and offers romantic connections. It also advises on
medical issues and advocacy activities. http://dimensionsmagazine.com.
Extra Hip is geared especially toward teens-of-size, offering tips on fashion
and advice on plus-size modeling. http://extrahip.com.
Naturally Thin is a discussion group, a positive community for naturally
thin women. http://community.livejournal.com.naturallythin.
On a Positive Note describes topics of interest to women-of-size such as
weight discrimination and self-esteem. http://largelypositive.com.

Without Measure is the representative zine for the International Size Acceptance Association (ISAA), offering activist news, health advice, and interviews. http://withoutmeasure.com.

Products for People-of-Size

Ample Stuff sells plus-size products such as seatbelt extenders, medical supplies, and fitness videos for people-of-size. http://amplestuff.com.
For plus-size clothing, see, among others, http://torrid.com, http://bandlu.com, http://bigbadbeautiful.com, and http://bandlu.com, http://bigbadbeautiful.com, and http://abigattitude.com.

Advice on Airline Seating for People-of-Size

Seat Guru explains airline seat dimensions. http://seatguru.com. See also the NAAFA site for air travel tips.

Notes

Introduction

1. Claudia Parsons, "NY Play 'Fat Pig' Tackles What May Be the Last Taboo." *Reuters*, http://www.reuters.com, December 25, 2004.

2. Advertisement for TheStreet.com, *New York Times Magazine* (August 27, 2000): 13.

3. Photo in *New York Times Magazine* (January 9, 2005): 16. The story is about college fraternity drinking and partying. The photo is of a shirt on the back of the president of Phi Delta Theta of Northwestern University.

4. Seen on a vehicle parked in the Tacoma Mall, Tacoma, Washington, May 7, 2002.

5. Naomi Wolf, *The Beauty Myth: How Images of Beauty Are Used against Women.* New York: Harper Perennial, 2002, p. 1.

6. Wolf, *The Beauty Myth*, p. 3.

7. Ibid.

8. Nancy Etcoff, *Survival of the Prettiest: The Science of Beauty.* New York: Anchor Books, 1999, p. 21.

9. Wolf, *The Beauty Myth*, p. 12.

10. Etcoff, *Survival of the Prettiest.*

11. Bonnie Berry, "The Power of Looks: An Historical Analysis of Social Aesthetics and Status Gain." Presented at the annual meeting of the Society for the Study of Social Problems, August 14, 2004. San Francisco, CA.

12. Etcoff, *Survival of the Prettiest*, pp. 139, 163.

13. Etcoff, *Survival of the Prettiest*, p. 32.

14. Sander L. Gilman, *Making the Body Beautiful: A Cultural History of Aesthetic Surgery.* Princeton, NJ: Princeton University, 1999, p. 24. For a comprehensive history of ugly law, see Susan Schweik's forthcoming book, *The Ugly Laws.* Her treatment covers a wide range of topics related to ugly law such as the overlap between the targets of ugly law and other minorities (women, African Americans, immigrants, the disabled, and the poor), the creation of the laws and the absence of enforcement, capitalism's influence on the need for such laws (to force beggars off the streets), and so on. Unsurprisingly, a major reason for the demise of ugly laws was sympathetic public response to the targeted victims of the laws, who were often disabled and always poor.

15. Virginia L. Blum, *Flesh Wounds: The Culture of Cosmetic Surgery.* Berkeley, CA: University of California, 2003, p. 141.

16. Charles Darwin, *The Descent of Man and Selection in Relation to Sex.* New York: Routledge, 1871.

17. Blum, *Flesh Wounds*, pp. 121–122.

18. Peter N. Stearns, *Fat History: Bodies and Beauty in the Modern West.* New York: New York University, 1997, pp. 3, 8.

19. Gina Kolata, "Some Extra Heft May Be Helpful, New Study Says." *New York Times* (April 20, 2005): A1, A20.

20. Cedric Herring, Verna M. Keith, and Hayward Derrick Horton (eds.), *Skin/Deep: How Race and Complexion Matter in the "Color-Blind" Era.* Chicago IL: University of Illinois, 2004. See also Etcoff, *Survival of the Prettiest*, pp. 115–119, 127–128.

21. In the 1890s, wealth, as symbolized by physical appearance, was represented by corpulence and financial failure as emaciation. In the twentieth century, innovations in agriculture and food processing allowed for cheaper, more abundant, and calorie-dense food, while labor-saving devices made sweat even scarcer. Because even working class and the poor could be fat under twentieth-century conditions, the elite in industrialized countries began to view thinness as a sign of high social status. As we now know, lower-income people are more likely to eat high-fat, calorie-dense food, and to not exercise. Much of the explanation for this class-weight difference has to do not only with differing value systems (say, a lack of interest in exercise) but also differing opportunities: the poorer quality of produce available in poor neighborhoods, the absence of safe places to walk, fewer recreational facilities, and stress that can lead to compulsive eating of fatty, sugary foods. See Natalie Angier, "Who Is Fat?" *New York Times* (November 7, 2000): D2.

22. Stearns, *Fat History*, p. vii.

23. Gilman, *Making the Body Beautiful.* The syphilitic nose was basically an absent or much-eaten-away nose. The Gilman book has a number of illustrations in the forms of drawings and one photograph of syphilitic noses. In the drawings of adult syphilitic noses, most of the bridge is missing due to the disease, such that the nostrils are cavernous; in the photograph of a noseless infant born with

congenital syphilis, the "nose" is merely a horizontal slit where the nostrils would be.

24. Debra L. Gimlin, *Body Work: Beauty and Self Image in American Culture.* Berkeley, CA: University of California, 2002, p. 5.

25. Stearn, *Fat History.* See also Mark V. Roehling, "Weight-Based Discrimination in Employment: Psychological and Legal Aspects." *Personnel Psychology* 52 (1999): 969–1016. In Roehling's review of studies of weight discrimination, he relies on court cases that use as their main standards for "recommended or ideal weight" the Metropolitan Life Insurance Company Height and Weight Tables and the Body Mass Index." See especially p. 970.

26. Marilyn Wann, *Fat!So?* Berkeley, CA: Ten Speed Press, 1998, p. 46.

27. A person who is "underweight" can also be considered abnormal. This person does not weigh "enough." See the size-acceptance Web site for a variety of size dimensions, height, and weight: http://www.size-acceptance.org.

28. Wann, *Fat!So?* p. 20

29. Sondra Solovay, *Tipping the Scales of Justice: Fighting Weight-Based Discrimination.* Amherst, NY: Prometheus, 2000, p. 29.

30. For a discussion of the functions of racism and sexism, see Bonnie Berry, *Social Rage: Emotion and Cultural Conflict.* New York: Garland/Taylor and Francis, 1999.

31. Gilman, *Making the Body Beautiful,* p. 108.

32. For Web sites on size-acceptance, see http://www.seaFATtle.org; http://www.naafa.org; http://www.size-acceptance.org.

Chapter 1

1. Nancy Etcoff, *Survival of the Prettiest: The Science of Beauty.* New York: Anchor, 1999.

2. Susan M. Alexander, "Stylish Hard Bodies: Branded Masculinity in Men's Health Magazine." *Sociological Perspectives* 46 (2003): 543.

3. Susan Bordo, *Unbearable Weight: Feminism, Western Culture and the Body.* Berkeley, CA: University of California, 1995; Naomi Wolf, *The Beauty Myth: How Images of Beauty Are Used against Women.* New York: Harper Perennial, 2002.

4. Gina Kolata, "What We Don't Know about Obesity." *New York Times* (June 22, 2003): 12, section 4.

5. I use the term "differently-abled" interchangeably with "disabled" to point out that those of us with mobility and other physical constraints are "able" even if not in the same light as those without such constraints.

6. Paul K. Longmore, personal communication, September 26, 2006.

7. Paul K. Longmore, *Why I Burned My Book and Other Essays on Disability.* Philadelphia, PA: Temple University, 2003.

8. Wendy Caldwell, "Half Naked." Sidelines Online: The Student Newspaper of Middle Tennessee State University, http://www.mtsusideliens.com, April 4, 2005.

9. Sarah Banet-Weiser, *The Most Beautiful Girl in the World: Beauty Pageants and National Identity*. Berkeley, CA: University of California, 1999.

10. Rob Stein, "Big, But Healthy." *Washington Post National Weekly Edition* (December 6–12, 2004): 31.

11. Kolata, "What We Don't Know about Obesity," p. 12.

12. Stein, "Big, But Healthy," p. 31.

13. Tracy Wheeler, "Can You Be Overweight But Fit?" *The Seattle Times*, http://www.seattletimes.com, August 3, 2003.

14. Paul Campos, "The Big Fat Con Story." *The Guardian*, http://www.guardian.co.uk, April 24, 2004; Paul Campos, *The Obesity Myth: Why America's Obsession with Weight is Hazardous to Your Health*. New York: Gotham Books, 2004.

15. Peter N. Stearns, Fat History: *Bodies and Beauty in the Modern West*. New York: New York University, 1997. In study after study on the looks-size topic, I find this concern with self-control rearing its ugly head, and not just among elites.

16. Gina Kolata, "Some Extra Heft May Be Helpful, New Study Says." *New York Times* (April 20, 2005): A1, A20.

17. Editors, "Study Shows Obesity Risks May Have Been Overstated." *Seattle Post-Intelligencer*, http://www.seattlepi.com), April 20, 2005.

18. Editors, "You Can Be Too Thin, After All." *New York Times* (April 22, 2005): A24.

19. Rob Stein, "Even a Few Extra Pounds Can Take Years Off Your Life, New Study Says." *The Seattle Times, http://www.seattletiems.nwsource.com, August 23, 2006; Carey Goldberg, "Even a Little Extra Fat May Shorten Lifespan." Seattle Post-Intelligencer*, http://www.seattlepi.nwsource.com, August 23, 2006.

20. Editors, "U.S. Warning on Death Toll from Obesity." *New York Times* (December 14, 2001): A21; Jane Brody, "Another Study Finds a Link between Excess Weight and Cancer." *New York Times* (May 6, 2003): D7; Editors, "Land of the Fat." *The Guardian*, http://www.guardian.co.uk, May 2, 2002.

21. Greg Critser, *Fatland*. Boston, MA: Houghton Mifflin, 2003; see esp. p. 109.

22. Howard Markel, "Dx: Supersize." *New York Times* (March 24, 2002): 4, section 4.

23. Gina Kolata, "While Children Grow Fatter, Experts Search for Solutions." *New York Times* (October 19, 2000): A1, A20.

24. Ibid.

25. Editors, "Are Our Children Becoming Couch Potatoes?" British Broadcasting Company, http://www.news.bbc.co.uk, February 21, 2002; Ronald Kotulak, "Obesity Giving Adult Illnesses to Kids." *Chicago Tribune*, http://www.chicagotribune.com, May 2, 2002.

26. Emma Ross, "Children Suffer Middle-Age Health Woes." *Seattle Post-Intelligencer*, http://www.seattlepi.com, June 1, 2005.

27. Kolata, "What We Don't Know about Obesity," p. 12 of Section 4. (See note 4.)

28. Gina Kolata, "For a World of Woes, We Blame Cookie Monsters." *New York Times* (October 29, 2006): 14, section 4.

29. Critser, *Fatland*; Gina Kolata, "No Days Off Are Allowed, Experts On Weight Argue." *New York Times* (October 18, 2000): A1, A18.

30. "Land of the Fat." *The Guardian*, May 2, 2002. (See note 17.) Beyond genes, it has also recently been suggested that viruses may be to blame for excess weight. See Robin Marantz Henig, "Fat Factors." *New York Times Magazine* (August 13, 2006): 28–57.

31. Critser, *Fatland*, pp. 27–28, 32–33, 41; Kolata, "No Days Off Are Allowed, Experts on Weight Argue." For example, fast food chains, wanting to make more money, increased portion size without significantly increasing the price, thus making the consumers feel that they were getting a good deal. Consumers did get a good economic deal (a lot of calories for their money), but they also put on weight. As another profit-motive example, food manufacturers wanting to make a larger profit chose "tree lard" (palm oil), hydrogenated fats, and corn syrup (all cheaply made) as key ingredients in prepared food instead of healthier fats and sugars.

32. Jean Renfro Anspaugh, *Fat Like Us*. Durham, NC: Windows on History, 2001.

33. Kim Chernin, *The Obsession: Reflections on the Tyranny of Slenderness*. New York: Harper and Row, 1981. As cited on p. 27 of Goodman (in note 30).

34. W. Charisse Goodman, *The Invisible Woman: Confronting Weight Prejudice in America*. Carlsbad, CA: Gurze, 1995, see esp. p. 139.

35. Editors, "You Can Be Too Thin, After All," p. A24. (See note 16.)

36. Sander L. Gilman, *Making the Body Beautiful: A Culture of Cosmetic Surgery*. Berkeley, CA: University of California, 2003, see esp. p. 231.

37. Ibid., pp. 207–208.

38. Marilyn Wann, *Fat! So?* Berkeley, CA: Ten Speed, 1998; Lara Frater, *Fat Chicks Rule: How to Survive in a Thin-Centric World*. Brooklyn, NY: IG, 2005.

39. Jana Evans Braziel and Kathleen Le Besco (eds.), *Bodies Out of Bounds; Fatness and Transgression*. Berkeley, CA: University of California, 2001, see esp. p. 7.

40. Ibid., p. 5.

41. Joyce L. Huff, "A 'Horror of Corpulence': Interrogating Bantingism and Mid-Nineteenth-Century Fat Phobia," pp. 39–59, in *Bodies Out of Bounds; Fatness and Transgression*, edited by J. E. Braziel and K. LeBesco. Berkeley, CA: University of California 2001, see esp. p. 47. See also Shelley Bovey, *The* Forbidden Body. London: Pandora, 1989.

42. Jacqueline Stenson, "Couch Potato Contentment." *MSNBC*, http://www.msnbc.com, February 8, 2005.

43. Critser, *Fatland*, p. 88.

44. Ibid., p. 90.

45. The Associated Press, "Americans Are More Accepting of Heavier Bodies." *MSNBC*, http://www.msnbc.com, January 11, 2006.

Chapter 2

1. Jean Renfro Anspaugh, *Fat Like Us*. Durham, NC: Windows on History, 2001.

2. Lucy Grealy, *Autobiography of a Face*. Boston, MA: Houghton Mifflin, 1994, see p. 150.

3. The author died at the age of 39 in 2002, of a drug overdose.

4. Nancy Etcoff, *Survival of the Prettiest: The Science of Beauty*. New York: Anchor, 1999, see pp. 65, 50.

5. Etcoff, *Survival of the Prettiest*, pp. 59, 61.

6. Ibid., p. 62.

7. Ibid.

8. Bonnie Berry, "Animal Aesthetics: Remaking Animals to Suit Our Image." *Animals and Society* 5(2004): 11–12. In this article, I discuss the attributional purpose served by our nonhuman companions. We want our animal companions to be special and beautiful, much as we do our children and romantic partners, partly if not largely because they then reflect well on us, their humans.

9. Etcoff, *Survival of the Prettiest*.

10. Ibid., p. 176.

11. Marilyn Wann, *Fat!So?* Berkeley, CA: Ten Speed, 1998, see pp. 59, 168.

12. Peter N. Stearns, *Fat History: Bodies and Beauty in the Modern West*. New York: New York University, 1997, see p. 71.

13. Ibid., p. 72.

14. Debra L. Gimlin, *Body Work: Beauty and Self Image in American Culture*. Berkeley, CA: University of California, 2002, see p. 111.

15. Ibid., p. 138.

16. Ibid., p. 132.

17. Ibid., p. 144.

18. Korie Edwards, Katrina M. Carter-Tellison, and Cedric Herring, "For Richer, For Poorer: Whether Dark or Light: Skin Tone, Marital Status, and Spouse's Earnings," pp. 65–81, in *Skin/Deep: How Race and Complexion Matter in the "Color-Blind" Era*, edited by C. Herring, V. M. Keith, and H. D. Horton. Chicago, IL: University of Illinois, 2004.

19. Wang Ping, *Aching for Beauty: Footbinding in China*. Minneapolis, MN: University of Minnesota, 2000, see p. 32.

20. Ibid., p. 41.

21. Etcoff, *Survival of the Prettiest*, p. 35.

22. Nicholas Bakalar, "Ugly Children May Get Parental Short Shrift." *New York Times* (May 3, 2005): D7.

23. Etcoff, *Survival of the Prettiest*, p. 37.

24. Editors, "Moms Have Double Standard for Fat Sons, Daughters." *Reuters*, http://www.reuters.com, May 5, 2003.

25. Ping, *Aching for Beauty*, p. 226.

26. Editors, "No Hunks in the Alcohol Advertisements, Please. We're British." *New York Times* (August 1, 2005): C4.

27. Melanie McFarland, *On TV:* "Ugly Betty" Tackles the Cruel Fashion World with Grace." *Seattle Post-Intelligencer*, http:www.seattlepi.nwsource.com, September 28, 2006; Virginia Heffernan, "A Plucky Guppy among the Barracudas." *New York Times* (September 28, 2006): B1, B8.

28. D. Parvaz, "If You're 40 but Look 30, Society Will See You Now." *Seattle Post-Intelligencer*, http://www.seattlepi.nwsource.com, May 31, 2005.

Chapter 3

1. Bonnie Berry (Chair), "Social Aesthetics: Public Reaction to Looks." Presented at the annual meeting of the Association for Humanist Sociology, November 13, 2004, Louisville, KY. The panelist, a graduate student, had just presented her research on the stigma attached to body mass. She and a fellow graduate student had conducted a study of weight stigma. To describe her own experience in the matter, she cited the severe social problems she had encountered because of her size, and admitted to having had bypass surgery to reduce her weight.

2. Maureen Dowd, "All That Glisters Is Gold." *New York Times* (May 4, 2005): A25.

3. Ibid., p. 25.

4. Nancy Etcoff, *Survival of the Prettiest: The Science of Beauty*. New York: Anchor Books, 1999; see p. 30 for quotation by Aristotle.

5. Mark V. Roehling, "Weight-Based Discrimination in Employment: Psychological and Legal Aspects." *Personnel Psychology* 52 (1999): 1002.

6. Gwendolyn Freed, "Matters of Size at Work." *Seattle Post Intelligencer*, http://www.seattlepi.nwsource.com, November 10, 2003.

7. Carey Goldberg, "Fat People Say an Intolerant World Condemns Them on First Sight." *New York Times* (November 5, 2000): A30.

8. Roehling, "Weight-Based Discrimination in Employment," pp. 982–983.

9. Ibid., p. 983.

10. Sondra Solovay, *Tipping the Scales of Justice: Fighting Weight-Based Discrimination*. Amherst, NY: Prometheus Books, 2000, see p. 103.

11. Peter N. Stearns, *Fat History: Bodies and Beauty in the Modern West*. New York: New York University, 1997, pp. 114–115.

12. Stearns, *Fat History*, p. 115.

13. Ibid., p. 117.

14. Robin Pogrebin, "Soprano Says Her Weight Cost Her Role in London." *New York Times* (March 9, 2004): B1. See also Editors, "It's All Over, Before 'Fat' Lady Sings Opera." *Reuters*, http://www.reuters.com, March 9, 2004.

15. Anthony Tommasini, "With Surgery, Soprano Sheds a Brunnhilde Body." *New York Times* (March 27, 2005): A1, A19.

16. Freed, "Matters of Size at Work." Another economic measure related to size is personal wealth, which ordinarily is accumulated from pay. According to a 2005 survey, based on a large U.S. sample and 15 years of data, both weight and weight fluctuations are related to our net worth. Heavy people have far less net worth than people who are not heavy (and who have the highest net worth). Heavy people who lose a significant amount of weight experience an increase in their personal wealth. Amy Norton, "People Who Lose Weight May Gain Wealth." *Reuters*, http://www.reuters.com, July 21, 2005.

17. Victoria Colliver, "Perils of Obesity Extend to Pay." *Seattle Post-Intelligencer*, http://www.seattlepi.nwsource.com, May 16, 2005.

18. Roehling, "Weight-Based Discrimination in Employment," p. 985.

19. Marilyn Wann, *Fat!So?* Berkeley, CA: Ten Speed, 1998, pp. 80, 126. Solovay, *Tipping the Scales of Justice*, p. 106.

20. Freed, "Matters of Size at Work"; Roehling, "Weight-Based Discrimination in Employment," p. 985.

21. Solovay, *Tipping the Scales of Justice*, p. 159.

22. Goldberg, "Fat People Say an Intolerant World Condemns Them on First Sight"; Solovay, *Tipping the Scales of Justice*.

23. Roehling, "Weight-Based Discrimination in Employment," pp. 991–992.

24. Ibid., p. 997.

25. Solovay, *Tipping the Scales of Justice*, p. 129.

26. Ibid., p. 130.

27. Ibid., pp. 130–131.

28. Ibid., p. 132.

29. Ibid., p. 129.

30. Jake Ellison, "Professor Fighting Discrimination Step by Step." *Seattle Post-Intelligencer*, http://www.seattlepi.nwsource.com, November 24, 2004. See also http://www.lpaonline.org or http://www.littlepeopleofamerica.org for information on Little People of America. LPA is a nonprofit advocacy group that numbers 24,000 members nationally, urging understanding and acceptance.

31. Etcoff, *Survival of the Prettiest*, p. 173.

32. Joseph Kahn, "Chinese People's Republic Is Unfair to Its Short People." *New York Times* (May 21, 2004): A15.

33. Steven Greenhouse, "Going for the Look, But Risking Discrimination." *New York Times* (July 13, 2003): 10.

34. Etcoff, *Survival of the Prettiest*, p. 63.

35. Ibid., p. 65.

36. Steven Greenhouse, "Refusal to Fire Unattractive Saleswoman Led to Dismissal, Suit Contends." *New York Times* (April 11, 2003): A10.

37. Greenhouse, "Refusal to Fire Unattractive Saleswoman Led to Dismissal, Suit Contends," p. A10, emphasis added.

38. Naomi Wolf, *The Beauty Myth: How Images of Beauty Are Used against Women*. New York: Harper Perennial, 2002, p. 21.

39. Ibid., p. 20: "... the power structure used the beauty myth materially to undermine the women's advancement."

40. Wolf, *The Beauty Myth*, p. 22.

41. Greenhouse, "Refusal to Fire Unattractive Saleswoman Led to Dismissal, Suit Contends," p. A10.

42. Steven Greenhouse, "Lifetime Affliction Leads to a U.S. Bias Suit." *New York Times* (March 30, 2003): A8.

43. Virginia Postrel, "Going to Great Lengths." *New York Times Magazine* (August 31, 2003): 16.

44. Solovay, *Tipping the Scales of Justice*, p. 104.

45. Etcoff, *Survival of the Prettiest*, p. 83.

46. Ibid., p. 83.

47. Teresa Riordan, *Inventing Beauty*. New York: Broadway Books, 2004, p. 190. See Thorstein Veblen, "The Economic Theory of Woman's Dress." *Popular Science Monthly* (December, 1984): 203.

48. Dowd, "All That Glisters Is Gold," p. A25.

49. Etcoff, *Survival of the Prettiest*, p. 84.

50. Wolf, *The Beauty Myth*, p. 39. This parallels a personal experience. In 1983, when I began my first post-Ph.D. position as an assistant professor, the department chair suggested that I wear dresses, skirts, pantyhose, heels, make-up, and "do something with your hair, honey." It came as quite a surprise to learn that a professor of the social sciences was expected to be sexually attractive to her colleagues.

51. Etcoff, *Survival of the Prettiest*, p. 56.

52. Roehling, "Weight-Based Discrimination in Employment," p. 1004.

53. Ibid., p. 1007.

54. Ibid., p. 1008.

55. Wolf, *The Beauty Myth*, p. 27. I urge the reader to consult Wolf pp. 27–57 for more on the PBQ, professional beauty qualification.

56. Wolf, *The Beauty Myth*, p. 28.

57. Ibid.

58. Ibid., p. 33.

59. Ibid., p. 36.

60. Ibid., p. 42.

Chapter 4

1. Milt Freudenheim, "Another Danger of Overweight." *New York Times* (May 27, 2005): C1, C6.

2. *Plastic Surgery Magazine*. 2002. Testimonials, p. 1.

3. *Prevention*. 2002.

4. Greg Critser, *Fatland*. Boston: Houghton Mifflin, 2003; see especially p. 52.

5. Jana Evans Braziel and Kathleen LeBesco (eds.), *Bodies Out of Bounds: Fatness and Transgression.* Berkeley, CA: University of California, 2001.

6. Richard Klein, "Fat Beauty," pp. 19–38, in *Bodies Out of Bounds*, edited by J. E. Braziel and K. LeBesco, see pp. 36–37.

7. Sondra Solovay, *Tipping the Scales of Justice: Fighting Weight-Based Discrimination.* Amherst, NY: Promotheus, 2000, see p. 203.

8. Critser, *Fatland*; Jean Renfro Anspaugh, *Fat Like Us.* Durham, NC: Windows on History, 2001; Gina Kolata, "No Days Off Are Allowed, Experts on Weight Argue." *New York Times* (October 18, 2000): A1, A18.

9. Hillel Schwartz, *Never Satisfied: A Cultural History of Diets, Fantasies, and Fat.* New York: Free Press, 1986; see especially p. 328.

10. Peter N. Stearns, *Fat History: Bodies and Beauty in the Modern West.* New York: New York University, 1997, p. 107.

11. Ibid., pp. 72–73.

12. Solovay, *Tipping the Scales of Justice*, p. 38.

13. Ibid., p. 28.

14. Ibid., pp. 186–187.

15. Amy Tan, "Diet Pill Ills Highlight Singapore's Slimness Mania." *Reuters*, http://www/reuters.com, June 10, 2002.

16. Kate Betts, "The Tyranny of Skinny, Fashion's Insider Secret." *New York Times* (March 31, 2002): 1, 8, section 9.

17. Braziel and LeBesco, *Bodies Out of Bounds*, p. 52. Braziel and LeBesco point out that the diet industry continually redefines the norm of what is fat and what is thin. Presently, we are instructed to be a size 0 if we want to look like a fashion model, instead of the fashion-model standard size 8 of not so long ago.

18. Betts, "The Tyranny of Skinny, Fashion's Insider Secret," p. 8.

19. Kolata, "No Days Off Are Allowed, Experts on Weight Argue," p. 1.

20. We also know that fat and thin people have some of the same eating behaviors: binge eating, skipping meals, and eating too quickly. All of these unhealthy eating habits typify behaviors of the obese and the thin. See, for example, p. 18 of Kolata, "No Days Off Are Allowed, Experts on Weight Argue." 2000.

21. Timothy Egan, "For Image-Conscious Boys, Steroids Are Powerful Lure." *New York Times* (November 22, 2002): A1, A22.

22. Egan, "For Image-Conscious Boys, Steroids Are Powerful Lure," p. 22.

23. Gina Kolata, Jere Longman, Tim Weiner, and Timothy Egan. "With No Answers On Risks, Steroid Users Still Say 'Yes.'" *New York Times* (December 12, 2002): A1, A19.

24. Kolata, Longman, Weiner, and Egan, "With No Answers on Risks, Steroid Users Still Say 'Yes,'" p. 19.

25. Associated Press, "Girls Are Abusing Steroids Too, Experts Say." Associated Press, http://www.msnbc.msn.com, April 25, 2005.

26. Natalie Angier, "Short Men, Short Shrift. Are Drugs the Answer?" *New York Times* (June 22, 2003): 12, section 4.

27. Stephen S. Hall, *Size Matters: How Height Affects the Health, Happiness, and Success of Boys—and the Men They Become*. New York: Houghton Mifflin, 2006.

28. Nancy Etcoff, *Survival of the Prettiest: The Science of Beauty*. New York: Anchor, 1999. See also Angier, "Short Men, Short Shrift. Are Drugs the Answer?" p. 12. In rebuke, department stores discovered in 2006 just how influential short women could be when they experimented with getting rid of petite clothing departments on the grounds that they were not needed. After a boycott, the department stores got the hint and restored the petite sections. See Michael Barbaro, "Where's the Petite Department? Going the Way of the Petticoat." *New York Times* (May 28, 2006): A1, A20.

29. John Schwartz, "The View from 5-Foot-3." *New York Times* (June 22, 2003): 12, section 4.

30. Virginia Postrel, "Going to Great Lengths." *New York Times Magazine* (August 31, 2003): 16.

31. I would interject that if they face limitations in athletic activities it may well be due to the limiting behavior of their playmates or supervising adults rather than real shortness-related limitations.

32. "Treating Kids' Short Stature Won't Up Self-Esteem." *Reuters*, http://www.reuters.com, July 3, 2002.

33. Deborah J. Burris-Kitchen. *Short Rage: An Autobiographical Look at Height-ism in America*. Santa Barbara, CA: Fithian Press, 2002.

34. Erica Reischer and Kathryn Koo, "The Body Beautiful." *Annual Review of Anthropology* 33 (2004): 297. Also, I am grateful to Prabha Unnithan of Colorado State University (personal communication, September 18, 2006) for information on marital status and Hindu women's cosmetic markings.

35. Postrel, "Going to Great Lengths," p. 29.

Chapter 5

1. Teresa Riordan, *Inventing Beauty*. New York: Broadway Books, 2004; Carol E. Lee. "It's Only May, and the Tanorexics Are Already Complaining." *New York Times* (May 13, 2005): A22.

2. Jessica Seigel, "Fat Chance." *New York Times* (August 15, 2005): A21.

3. Nancy Etcoff, *Survival of the Prettiest; The Science of Beauty*. New York: Anchor, 1999, see p. 96.

4. Wikipedia. Available from World Wide Web: http://en.wikipedia.org. See also the U.S. Food and Drug Administration's Food, Drug, and Cosmetic Act, which defines drugs as "those products that cure, treat, mitigate, or prevent disease or that affect the structure or function of the human body. While the drugs are subject to an intensive review and approval process by FDA, cosmetics are not approved by FDA prior to sale," http://www.cfsan.fda.gov.

5. Wikipedia. Other definitions are found on Google and are as follows: Cos-meceuticals are "nutritionally enriched ingredients that are used in natural and

fortified cosmetic applications for a planned and specific way to achieve a desired result with a 100% naturally processed and composed item." Cosmeceuticals are products "formulated to improve the skin's health and appearance, they may also have positive physiological effects on the skin on a cellular level (antioxidants, for example)." Cosmeceuticals are skin treatments that provide "added benefit beyond a simple cosmetic or moisturizer." Cosmeceuticals are "skin care products that contain vital nutrients, which combat the damage of free-radicals and reduce inflammation, keeping skin in a youthful condition." Cosmeceuticals are "topical cosmetic pharmaceutical hybrids intended to enhance the health and beauty of the skin and body," http://www.google.com; http://www.milnefruit.com; http://www.celltechpersonalcare.com; http://www.naturalskinandhair.com; http://www.zonecafe.com; http://www.milnefruit.com; http://www.celltechpersonalcare.com; http://www.naturalskinandhair.com; http://www.zonecafe.com; http://www.egoscience.ch/dictionary.html.

6. Virginia Postrel, *The Substance of Style*. New York: HarperCollins, 2003, see p. 30.

7. Shari Roan, "Ciao, Collagen! Farewell, Face-Lift! It's Filler Time!" *The Seattle Times*, http://www.seattletimes.nwsource.com, September 3, 2006. Dermal fillers are injected substances that smooth out wrinkles and plump up depressions and crevasses in the skin. The effects last 6 months to many (as much as 8) years, not uncommonly lasting 2 to 5 years; thus, they are referred to as permanent or semipermanent procedures. The fillers, depending on the manufacturer, consist of synthetic materials, hyaluronic acid (found naturally in the body's connective tissue), human fat, human collagen, bovine collagen, or combinations of these materials.

8. Riordan, *Inventing Beauty*, p. xvii.

9. Ibid., pp. xviii, xix.

10. Erica Reischer and Kathryn Koo, "The Body Beautiful: Symbolism and Agency in the Social World." *Annual Review of Anthropology* 33 (2004): 297–317, see p. 298. Reischer and Koo cite Sander Gilman, *Making the Body Beautiful: A Cultural History of Aesthetic Surgery.* Princeton, NJ: Princeton University, 1999, see p. 4.

11. Etcoff, *Survival of the Prettiest*, pp. 95, 191.

12. Seigel, "Fat Chance," p. A21.

13. James Gorman, "Plastic Surgery Gets a New Look" *New York Times* (April 27, 2004): D1, D6. On eyelash extensions, see Gerit Quealy, "Lashes That Flirt and Flutter, But at What Cost?" *New York Times* (December 7, 2006): E3.

14. Postrel, *The Substance of Style*, p. 30.

15. Riordan, *Inventing Beauty*, p. 204.

16. Ibid., pp. 235, 261.

17. Ibid., p. 236.

18. British Broadcasting Company, *India Debates 'Racist' Skin Cream Ads.* British Broadcasting Company, http://www.bbc.co.uk, July 24, 2003.

19. Marc Lacey, "Fighting 'Light Skin' as a Standard of Beauty." *New York Times* (June 15, 2002): A4. See also Sally Wadyka, "Trouble Spots Got You Down? Lighten Up." *New York Times* (July 21, 2005): E3. Wadyka tells us that skin lighteners are not just racial; they can be used for correcting mottled skin. Whatever their purposes, they are dangerous.

20. Cedric Herring, Verna M. Keith, and Hayward Derrick Horton (eds.), *Skin/Deep: Race and Complexion in the Color-Blind Era*. Chicago, IL: University of Illinois, 2004; see Chapter 1 by Cedric Herring, pp. 1–21, especially p. 7.

21. Lee, "It's Only May, and the Tanorexics Are Already Complaining," p. A22.

22. Ibid. See also Karen Springen, "Dying to Be Tan." *MSNBC*, http://www.msnbc.msn.com, June 28, 2005. Springen discusses the effects of tanning on the young who feel that looking sexy right now is more important than health hazards in their mid-40s.

23. Enid Schildkrout, "Inscribing the Body." *Annual Review of Anthropology* 33 (2004): 319–344. I'll say more about scarification in the next chapter.

24. Etcoff, *Survival of the Prettiest*, p. 100.

25. Susan Bordo, *Unbearable Weight: Feminism, Western Culture and the Body*. Berkeley, CA: University of California, 1995, see p. 162, emphasis mine. See also Amaury deRiencourt, *Sex and Power in History*. New York: David McKay, 1974.

26. Postrel, *The Substance of Style*, p. 29.

27. Ibid., p. 28.

28. Etcoff, *Survival of the Prettiest*, p. 129.

29. Riordan, *Inventing Beauty*, p. 120.

30. Quealy, "Lashes That Flirt and Flutter, But at What Cost?" p. 3.

31. Kelly Yamanouchi, *A Cosmetic Change: Men Belly Up to the Makeup Bar*. Chicago Tribune, http://www.chicagotribune.com, May 8, 2002.

32. Susan M. Alexander, "Stylish Hard Bodies: Branded Masculinity in *Men's Health Magazine*." *Sociological Perspectives* 46 (2003): 550.

33. Yamanouchi, *A Cosmetic Change*.

34. Hilary Claggett, personal communication, 2005. I credit Ms. Claggett, editor at Praeger/Greenwood, for the notion of and term "Botox Nation."

Chapter 6

1. Patrick Healy, "Flaunting the Face of Cosmetic Surgery (and a Few Other Parts as Well)." *New York Times* (October 23, 2003): C18.

2. Susan Saulny, "After Cosmetic Surgery, the 'Do Over.'" *New York Times* (August 4, 2005): E1, E2.

3. James Gorman, "Plastic Surgery Gets a New Look." *New York* Times (April 27, 2004): D1, D6.

4. Virginia Postrel, *The Substance of Style*. New York: HarperCollins, 2003, see p. 30.

5. Sander L. Gilman, *Making the Body Beautiful: A Cultural History of Aesthetic Surgery*. Princeton, NJ: Princeton University, 1999.

6. Virginia L. Blum, *Flesh Wounds: The Culture of Cosmetic Surgery*. Berkeley, CA: University of California, 2003, see p. 9.

7. Gilman, *Making the Body Beautiful*, p. 4.

8. Ibid., p. 8.

9. Ibid., p. 157.

10. Brenda Fowler, "Face Forward." *New York Times Magazine* (May 5, 2002): 98.

11. Craig S. Smith, "Dire Wounds, a New Face, a Glimpse in the Mirror." *New York* Times (December 3, 2005): A1, A6. In Lyons, France on November 26–27, 2005, a partial transplant was taken from a brain-dead woman and attached to the damaged face of the patient. The full-face transplant involves a 24-hour surgery, lifting an entire face usually from a dead donor (including nose cartilage, nerves, and muscles) and transferring this face to the disfigured face. One issue raised by this new procedure is that of identity, with a key question being whether the patients can come to terms with their new appearance. The counterargument is that they have to come to terms with an altered appearance anyway, from the disfigurement or from grafts and other repairs, and the surgery is expected to help disfigured patients regain normal lives. Another, more medical, issue is that the patient's immune system may reject the new face. See also Tim Radford, "Scientists Prepare to Turn Fiction into Fact with First Full-Face Transplant." *The Guardian*, http://www.guardian.co.uk, May 27, 2004; Michael Mason, "A New Face." *New York Times* (July 26, 2005): D1, D6.

12. Psychological consequences experienced by the patients who have had transplants from dead or brain-dead donors are not insignificant. A man who had a dead person's hand transplanted in place of his own had the transplanted hand amputated because he had become "mentally detached" from the "hideous and withered" hand, even though the hand was operational. See Ian Sample, "Man Rejects First Penis Transplant." *The Guardian*, http://www.guardian.co.uk, September 18, 2006.

13. Gina Kolata, "Longing to Lose, at a Cost." *New York* Times (January 4, 2005): D6.

14. Denise Grady, "Exchanging Obesity's Risks for Surgery's." *New York Times* (October 12, 2000): A1, A24.

15. Teresa Riordan, *Inventing Beauty: A History of the Innovations that Have Made Us Beautiful*. New York: Broadway Books, 2004, see p. 110.

16. Blum, *Flesh Wounds*, p. 75.

17. Healy, "Flaunting the Face of Cosmetic Surgery," p. 18: these are 2002 figures. See also Blum, *Flesh Wounds*, p. 87; Debra Gimlin, *Body Work: Beauty and Self-Image in American Culture*. Berkeley, CA: University of California, 2002, p. 75.

18. British Broadcasting Company, "Shanghai Men Seek Chest Implants." *BBC News*, http://bbc.co.uk, October 14, 2004.

19. William McCall, "Nip, Tuck, Shot... More Men Are Using Cosmetic Surgery." *Seattle Post-Intelligencer*, http://www. seattlepi.nwsource.com, January 6, 2005. Besides the increasing use of cosmetic surgery by men, they are also increasingly succumbing to eating disorders and have "never been immune to the persuasions of the multibillion-dollar diet and beauty industries," according to Jerry Mosher. See Jerry Mosher, 2001. "Setting Free the Bears: Refiguring Fat Men on Television," pp. 166–193 (especially p. 167) in *Bodies Out of Bounds: Fatness and Transgression*, edited by J. E. Braziel and K. LeBesco. Berekeley, CA: University of California. Men are becoming vulnerable to "the same image-centered social forces that have for so long oppressed women," as seen not only in the rise of surgeries but also the plethora of men's lifestyle magazines," according to Blum, *Flesh Wounds*, p. 48.

20. Gilman, *Making the Body Beautiful*, pp. 32, 33.

21. James Gorman, "Plastic Surgery Gets a New Look." *New York Times* (April 27, 2004): D1, D6.

22. Gilman, *Making the Body Beautiful*, p. 16.

23. Erica Reischer and Kathryn S. Koo, "The Body Beautiful: Symbolism and Agency in the Social World." *Annual Review of Anthropology* 33 (2004): 297–317, see especially p. 305. See also Gilman, *Making the Body Beautiful*, pp. 85–118.

24. Gilman, *Making the Body Beautiful*, p. 116.

25. Ibid., p. 111.

26. Ibid., pp. 114–115, 117.

27. Ibid., p. 105.

28. Ibid., pp. 106, 108.

29. E. Kaw, "'Opening' Faces: the Politics of Cosmetic Surgery and Asian American Women," pp. 241–265, in *Many Mirrors: Body Image and Social Relations*, edited by N. Sault. New Brunswick, NJ: Rutgers University, 1994. See also Reischer and Koo, "The Body Beautiful," p. 305.

30. Blum, *Flesh Wounds*, p. 10.

31. Ibid., p. 10.

32. Gilman, *Making the Body Beautiful*, p. 26; see also pp. 295–296.

33. Stephen G. Henderson, "Expect a Few Upturned Noses After Your Facelift." *The Seattle Times*, http://www.seattletimes.nwsource.com, December 14, 2005.

34. Nancy Etcoff. *Survival of the Prettiest: The Science of Beauty*. New York: Anchor Books, 1999, see p. 112.

35. James Gorman, "Different Sizes for Different Regions." *New York Times* (April 27, 2004): D6.

36. Guy Trebay, "Curb Appeal: Seduction from the Ground Up." *New York Times* (June 17, 2003): C20.

37. Gardiner Harris, "If Shoe Won't Fit, Fix the Foot? Popular Surgery Raises Concern." *New York Times* (December 7, 2003): A1, A24.

38. Harris, "If Shoe Won't Fit, Fix the Foot?" pp. A1, A24.

39. As with all plastic surgery, bear in mind that this form of medical practice is almost strictly a cash business and not covered by managed care. See Trebay, "Curb Appeal: Seduction from the Ground Up," p. C20, and Harris, "If Shoe Won't Fit, Fix the Foot? Popular Surgery Raises Concern," p. A24.

40. From a feminist perspective, this remark immediately begs the question of why women want to be whistled at. Being whistled at could more accurately be viewed as a form of sexual harassment rather than a compliment. Also, it bears pointing out here that it is not just that the surgery can cause injury, the shoes themselves can lead to severe foot problems as well as knee, pelvic, back, and shoulder pain. Heel height is part of the problem but so is the fact that "almost 90 percent of women routinely wear shoes that are one or two sizes too narrow," writes Harris in "If Shoe Won't Fit, Fix the Foot? Popular Surgery Raises Concern," p. A24.

41. Craig Smith, "Risking Limbs for Height, and Success, in China." *New York Times* (May 5, 2002): A3.

42. Dan Hurley, "Does He Or Doesn't He? It's Harder to Tell." *New York Times* (June 15, 2004): D1, D6.

43. Julie Scelfo, "Eyelash Transplants Grow in Popularity." *MSNBC*, http://www.msnbc.msn.com,November 18, 2006.

44. Reuters, "Doctors: Penis Enlargement Surgery No Help." *MSNBC*, http://www.msnbc.msn.com,February 14, 2006.

45. Sample, "Man Rejects First Penis Transplant."

46. Gorman, "Different Sizes for Different Regions," p. D1.

47. Ibid., p. D6.

48. Natasha Singer, "Do My Knees Look Fat to You?" *New York Times* (June 15, 2006): 1, 3, section E.

49. Curran Smith, personal communication, MD, Seattle, Washington, 2001. See also plastic surgery Web sites: http://www.seattledocs.com; http://www.uwcosmeticsurgery.org.

50. Christine Lennon, "A Cure for Cellulite? Some Doctors Say 'Fat Chance,'" http://www.seattlepi.nwsource.com, June 16, 2005.

51. Alex Johnson, "Cosmetic Surgery's Bright, Shiny New Face." *MSNBC*, http://www.msnbc.msn.com, August 2, 2005.

52. Marilyn Yalom, *A History of the Breast.* New York: Knopf, 1997.

53. Riordan, *Inventing Beauty*, p. 278.

54. Yalom, *A History of the Breast.* See also Alex Kuczynski, "A Lovelier You, with Off-the-Shelf Parts." *New York Times* (May 2, 2004): 1, 12, section 4.

55. Alex Kuczynski, "If Beauties Multiply, They'll Be Plain to See." *New York Times* (December 28, 2003): 4, section 4.

56. Susan Bordo, *Unbearable Weight: Feminism, Western Culture, and the Body.* Berkeley, CA: University of California, 1995, see p. 162.

57. Louise J. Kaplan, *Female Perversions: The Temptations of Emma Bovary.* Northvale, NJ: Jason Aronson, 1997; see also Blum, *Flesh Wounds*, p. 287.

58. William Saletan, *Among the Transhumanists*. Slate, http://www.slate.com, August 28, 2006.

59. Steven Van Wolputte, "Hang on to Your Self: Of Bodies, Embodiment, and Selves." *Annual Review of Anthropology* 33 (2004): 251–269. For the definitive statement of the social mirror, see also George Herbert Mead, *Mind, Self and Society*. Chicago, IL: University of Chicago, 1974.

60. Susan Bordo, "'Material Girl': the Effacement of Postmodern Culture." *Michigan Quarterly Review* 29 (1990): 657.

61. Joan Finklestein, *The Fashioned Self*. Philadelphia, PA: Temple University, 1991, see p. 87.

Chapter 7

1. Reed Abelson, "Dental Double Standards." *New York Times* (December 28, 2004): C1–C5, see especially C1.

2. Ibid., p. C5.

3. Marilyn Wann, *Fat! So?* Berkeley, CA: Ten Speed Press, 1998, see pp. 78–79.

4. Paul K. Longmore, *Why I Burned My Book and Other Essays on Disability*. Philadelphia, PA: Temple University, 2003, see pp. 21, 204–205.

5. Joyce L. Huff, "A 'Horror of Corpulence': Interrogating Bantingis, and Mid-Nineteenth-Century Fat-Phobia," pp. 39–59, in *Bodies Out of Bounds: Fatness and Transgression*, edited by J. E. Braziel and K. Le Besco. Berkeley, CA: University of California, 2001; see especially p. 46.

6. Mark. V. Roehling, "Weight-Based Discrimination in Employment: Psychological and Legal Aspects." *Personnel Psychology* 52 (1999): 969–1016, see p. 970.

7. Peter N. Stearns, *Fat History: Bodies and Beauty in the Modern West*. New York: New York University, 1997, see p. 111.

8. Ibid.

9. Huff, "A 'Horror of Corpulence,'" p. 47; see also Stearns, *Fat History*.

10. Wann, *Fat!So?* p. 10.

11. Patricia Reaney, "Health Costs of Obesity Exceed Smoking and Drinking." *Reuters*, http://www.reuters.com, June 3, 2005. Kim Dixon, "Smokers, Obese Should Pay More Health Insurance: Poll." *Reuters*, http://www.reuters.com, November 14, 2006.

12. Reaney, "Health Costs of Obesity Exceed Smoking and Drinking."

13. Stearns, *Fat History*, p. 45.

14. Sondra Solovay, *Tipping the Scales of Justice: Fighting Weight-Based Discrimination*. Amherst, NY: Prometheus Books, 2000, see p. 189.

15. British Broadcasting Company, "Fat Equals Lazy, Say Doctors." *BBC News*, http://www.newsvotebbc.co.uk, September 27, 2003.

16. Bonnie Berry, "Social Aesthetics: Reconstructions of Body Size." Presented at the annual meeting of the Society for the Study of Social Problems, August 13, 2005, Philadelphia, PA.

17. Wann, *Fat!So?* p. 33.

18. Ibid., p. 35.

19. Ibid., p. 36.

20. Milt Freudenheim, "Another Danger of Overweight." *New York Times* (May 27, 2005): C1, C2.

21. Ibid., p. C1.

22. Susan Levine, "Super-Size Medical Care Grows." *MSNBC*, http://www.msnbc.msn.com, January 3, 2006.

23. Edwin Black, *War against the Weak: Eugenics and America's Campaign to Create a Master Race.* London: Four Walls Eight Windows, 2003, see p. 432.

24. Ibid., p. 433.

25. Ibid., p. 436.

Chapter 8

1. Jake Ellison, "Professor Fighting Discrimination Step by Step." *Seattle Post-Intelligencer*, http://www.seattlepi.nwsource.com, November 24, 2004.

2. Naomi Wolf, *The Beauty Myth: How Images of Beauty Are Used against Women.* New York: Harper Perennial, 2002, see p. 11.

3. Mark. V. Roehling, "Weight-Based Discrimination in Employment: Psychological and Legal Aspects." *Personnel Psychology* 52 (1999): 969–1016; see p. 988.

4. Ibid., p. 990.

5. Ibid., p. 989.

6. Ibid., p. 988.

7. Ibid., pp. 988–989.

8. Ibid., p. 991.

9. Patricia Leigh Brown, "Jazzercise Relents to Plus-Size Pressure." *New York Times* (May 8, 2002): A18.

10. British Broadcasting Company, "Fighting for the Right to Be Fat." *BBC News*, http://www.bbc.co.uk, March 5, 2002.

11. "Fat Man Sues McDonald's Over Non-Hire." *The Seattle Times*, http://www.seattletimes.nwsource.com,April 17, 2003. Confusingly, in 2003, Mr. Connor charged that McDonald's wrongly concluded that he is disabled. See Steven Greenhouse, "Overweight, but Ready to Make a Case in Court." *New York Times* (August 4, 2003): A13.

12. Marilyn Wann, *Fat! So?* Berkeley, CA: Ten Speed Press, 1998, see p. 154.

13. Debra L. Gimlin, *Body Work: Beauty and Self-Image in American Culture.* Berkeley, CA: University of California, 2002, see p. 127.

14. Evelyn Nieves, "San Francisco Ordinance Outlaws Size Discrimination." *New York Times* (May 9, 2000): A16.

15. I urge the reader to consult the airlines for these polices or check Lara Frater's list of airlines and seating rules. Lara Frater, *Fat Chicks Rule! How to Survive in a Thin-Centric World.* Brooklyn, NY: IG publisher, 2005, see pp. 92–93.

16. Joe Sharkey, "Think You're Cramped? Try Coach at 400 Pounds." *New York Times* (February 15, 2005): C9.

17. Abby Ellin, "Tough for the Thin, Tougher for the Hefty." *New York Times* (February 15, 2005): C9.

18. Jon Herskovitz, "Passengers of Size" Pay Double on Southwest." *Reuters,* http://www.reuters.com, June 20, 2002.

19. British Broadcasting Company, "Crushed Flier Wins Obesity Payout." *BBC News,* http://www.bbc.co.uk, October 21, 2002.

20. Susan Schweik, *The Ugly Laws.* New York: New York University Press, forthcoming.

Chapter 9

1. Naomi Wolf. *The Beauty Myth.* New York: HarperPerennial, 2002, p. 12.

2. Nancy Etcoff, *Survival of the Prettiest.* New York: Anchor Press, 1999, p. 137.

3. Larry Rohter, "Beaches for the Svelte, Where the Calories Are Showing." *New York Times* (January 13, 2005): A4. Sander Gilman, "Ethnicity and Aesthetic Surgery," pp. 110–135, in *Aesthetic Surgery,* edited by A. Taschen. Koln, Germany: Taschen, 2005.

4. Henri E. Cauvin, "South Africa Confronts Another Health Problem: Obesity." *New York Times* (December 19, 2000): D1, D6.

5. Ellen Ruppel Shell, "New World Syndrome." *The Atlantic Monthly,* 287(6) (2001): 50–53, see especially p. 50.

6. Ibid., p. 52.

7. Ibid., p. 53.

8. Ibid., p. 53.

9. Seth Mydans, "Clustering in Cities, Asians Are Becoming Obese." *New York Times* (March 13, 2003): A3.

10. Greg Critser, "Now It's the Big Fat French Life." *New York Times* (May 18, 2003): 7, Section 4.

11. Paul Krugman,"Girth of a Nation." *New York Times* (July 4, 2005): A17.

12. Greg Critser, *Fatland.* New York: Houghton Mifflin, 2003, see p. 139.

13. Ibid., pp. 10–11.

14. Ibid., pp. 14–15.

15. Erica Goode, "The Gorge-Yourself Environment." *New York Times* (July 22, 2003): D1, D7.

16. Critser, *Fatland.*

17. Ibid., pp. 20–21.

18. Ibid., pp. 21, 23.

19. Greg Winter, "States Attempt to Curb Sales of Soda and Candy in Schools." *New York Times* (September 9, 2001): A1, A26.

20. Critser, *Fatland*, p. 47.

21. Ibid., p. 48.

22. Melanie Warner, "Striking Back at the Food Police." *New York Times* (June 12, 2005): 1, 9, Section 3.

23. Associated Press, "Manufacturers Supersize Stretchers." *MSNBC*, http://www.msnbc.com, October 19, 2003.

24. Dave Scheiber, "Companies Super-Size Products to Fit a Growing Public's Need." *Seattle Post-Intelligencer*, http://www.seattlepi.nwsource.com, October 27, 2003.

24. See also Margaret Webb Pressler, "Companies Learn There's Money to Be Made in Accommodating Extra-Wide Americans." *Washington Post National Weekly Edition* (November 24—30, 2003): 19.

25. Jui Chakravorty, "Catering to Obese Becoming Big Business." *Reuters*, http://www.reuters.com, October 4, 2003. See also "Taking Measures of Our Bodies . . . and Ourselves." *New York Times* (June 22, 2003): 12, Section 4.

26. Jean Renfro Anspaugh, *Fat Like Us*. Durham, NC: Windows on History Press, 2001.

27. Stephanie Saul, "Penny-Wise, Not Pound Foolish." *New York Times* (May 19, 2005): C1, C13.

28. Michael Erman, "Big Kids' Clothing Becoming Big Business." *Reuters*, http://www.reuters.com, August 3, 2002.

29. Suzanne D'Amato, "Young Women Face Fashion's Larger Problem." *The Washington Post*, http://www.msnbc.com, May 31, 2005.

30. Ginia Bellafante, "Young and Chubby: What's Heavy about That?" *New York Times* (January 26, 2003): 1, 2, Section 9.

31. Susan M Alexander, "Stylish Hard Bodies: Branded Masculinity in *Men's Health* Magazine." *Sociological Perspectives* 46(4) (2003): 535–554; see p. 535.

32. Ibid., p. 550.

33. Ibid., p. 552.

34. As documented by the National Education Association and as noted in Sondra Solovay, *Tipping the Scales of Justice*. Amherst, NY: Prometheus Books, 2000; see p. 33.

35. Solovay, *Tipping the Scales of Justice*, p. 26.

36. Ibid.

37. Ibid.

38. Critser, *Fatland*, p. 69.

39. Ibid., p. 70.

40. Ibid., p. 73.

41. Virginia L. Blum, *Flesh Wounds: The Culture of Cosmetic Surgery*. Berkeley, CA: University of California, 2003, see p. 132.

42. Wolf, *The Beauty Myth* [1991 edition], p. 28. As found in Erica Reischer and Kathryn S. Koo, "The Body Beautiful: Symbolism and Agency in the Social World." *Annual Review of Anthropology* 33 (2004): 297–317; see pp. 301–302.

43. Sarah Banet-Weiser, *The Most Beautiful Girl in the World*. Berkeley, CA: University of California, 1999, see pp. 3, 21. Using the Miss America contest as an illustration, Banet-Weiser notes that women's beauty can be viewed as a commodity, as something sellable, and as a conduit to sell other products via advertising.

44. Etcoff, *Survival of the Prettiest*, p. 6; Wolf, *The Beauty Myth*, p. 17. Wolf, in the 2002 edition, reminds us that financially powerful industries are involved: we spend $33 billion dollars annually on the diet industry, $20 billion on cosmetics, and $300 million on cosmetic surgery.

Chapter 10

1. Naomi Wolf, The Beauty Myth: How Images of Beauty Are Used against Women. New York: Harper Perennial, 2002, p. 8.

2. Leanne Libert, "Window-Shopping on New York's Fifth Avenue Reveals a New Shape and Style in Fashion" *National NOW Times* (Winter 2004–2005): 16. The Associated Press, "Dove Ads with 'Real' Women Get Attention." *MSNBC*, http://www.msnbc.msn.com, July 31, 2005.

3. Susanna Schrobsdorff, "Summer of Dove." *MSNBC*, http://www.msnbc. msn.com, August 3, 2005. See also the Dove Web site, http://www. campaignforrealbeauty.com.

4. Samantha Barbas, "No Soap to the Real-Beauty Pitch." *Seattle Post Intelligencer*, http://www.seattlepi.nwsource.com, August 18, 2005.

5. Eric Wilson, "When Is Thin Too Thin?" *New York Times* (September 21, 2006): E1, E7; "Where Size 0 Doesn't Make the Cut." *New York Times* (September 22, 2006): A20; "India Adds Its Weight to Thin Model Debate." *Reuters*, http:www.reuters.com, September 19, 2006; Ben Harding, "Madrid Enforces Skinny Models Ban." *Reuters*, http:www.reuters.com, September 18, 2006; Associated Press, "British Minister Says Ban Scrawny Models." *Seattle Post-Intelligencer*, http://www.seattlepi.nwsource.com, September 16, 2006; Alexi Mostrous and Hugh Muir, "Jowell Joins Condemnation of 'Stick-Thin' Catwalk Models." *The Guardian*, http://www.politics.guardian.co.uk, September 16, 2006; Rachel Sanderson, "Skinny Model Storm Hits London Fashion Week." *Reuters*, http://www.reuters.com, September 15, 2006; Andrew Hay, "Spain Ban on Skinny Models Shocks Fashion World." *Reuters*, http://www.reuters.com, September 12, 2006; Associated Press, "Italy Adopts New Rules on Thin Models." *MSNBC*, http://www. msnbc.msn.com, December 23, 2006.

6. Elizabeth Weil, "Heavy Questions." *New York Times Magazine* (January 2, 2005): 34–39.

7. Jacqueline Stenson, "Couch Potato Contentment." *MSNBC*, http://www.msnbc.msn.com, February 8, 2005. See also Bonnie Berry, "Social Aesthetics: Reconstructions of Body Size." Presented at the annual meetings of the Society for the Study of Social Problems, Philadelphia, PA, August 13, 2005.

8. The Associated Press, "Americans Are More Accepting of Heavier Bodies." *MSNBC*, http://www.msnbc.msn.com, January 11, 2006.

9. Ibid.

10. Lara Frater, *Fat Chicks Rule*. Brooklyn, NY: IG Publishing, 2006. See also Chapter 9 herein.

11. Anthony Ramirez, "Getting Old, Miss America Is Dropped by Network. There Is No Runner-Up." *New York Times* (October 21, 2004): A26. See also Jeffery Gettleman, "There She Goes, Miss America." *New York Times* (August 26, 2005): A17.

12. Jon Hurdle, "As Ratings Fall, Miss America Succumbs to Reality." *Reuters*, http://www.reuters.com, April 29, 2005.

13. Wolf, *The Beauty Myth*, p. 4.

14. Susan Bordo, *Unbearable Weight: Feminism, Western Culture, and the Body*. Berkeley, CA: University of California, 1995, p. 25.

15. Ibid., pp. 24–25.

16. Edwin Black, *War against the Weak: Eugenics and America's Campaign to Create a Master Race*. New York: Four Walls Eight Windows, 2003, p. 442.

17. Ibid., pp. 442–443.

18. Greg Critser, *Fatland*. New York: Houghton Mifflin, 2003, p. 60.

19. Ibid., pp. 91–92.

20. Deborah Haynes, "Age No Barrier to Anorexia, Illness Afflicts Children." *Reuters*, http://www.reuters.com, December 4, 2006; Michelle Nichols, "Anorexia, Bulimics Learn Methods Online: Study." *Reuters*, http://www.reuters.com, December 4, 2006; Karen Springen, "Study Looks at Pro-Anorexia Web Sites." *Newsweek*, http://www.msnbc.msn.com December 8, 2006.

21. Wang Ping, *Aching for Beauty: Footbinding in China*. Minneapolis, MN, University of Minnesota, 2000; see also Chapter 6 herein on plastic surgery. For remarks on historical changes in women's aesthetic pursuits, from Victorian ages to present day, see Joan Jacobs Brumberg, *The Body Project: An Intimate History of American Girls*. New York: Vintage, 1998.

22. Jana Evans Braziel and Kathleen LeBesco, *Bodies Out of Bounds: Fatness and Transgression*. Berkeley, CA: University of California, 2001, p. 2. See also Berry, "Social Aesthetics," cited in note 7.

23. Ibid., pp. 2–3, 136. See also Le'a Kent, "Fighting Abjection," pp. 130–150, in *Bodies Out of Bounds: Fatness and Transgression*, edited by J. E. Braziel and K. Le Besco. Berkeley, CA: University of California, 2001. See also Vivian Mayer, Foreword of *Shadow on a Tightrope: Writings by Women on Fat Oppression*, edited by Lisa Schoenfielder and Barb Weiser, Iowa City, IA: Aunt Lute, 1983.

24. Marilyn Wann, *Fat!So?* Berkeley, CA: Ten Speed Press, 1998, p. 168.

25. See Frater, *Fat Chicks Rule*, pp. 100–102 for a list and description of fat-advocacy groups. See also SeaFATtle, http://www.seafattle.org, National Association to Advance Fat Acceptance, http://www.naafa.org, International Size Acceptance Association, http://www.size-acceptance.org.

26. These laws are not dissimilar to "Jim Crow" laws of the Southern U.S. prohibiting African Americans venturing forth any place they chose and the Nazi prohibitions against Jews entering public parks. Sander L. Gilman, *Making the Body Beautiful: A Cultural History of Aesthetic Surgery*. Princeton, NJ: Princeton University, 1999, p. 24. See also Susan Schweik, *The Ugly Laws*. New York: New York University Press, forthcoming.

27. Alessandra Stanley, "Prime Time Gets Real with a Plump Heroine." *New York Times* (October 8, 2002): B1, B6. See also Camryn Manheim, *Wake Up, I'm Fat*. New York: Broadway Books, 1999.

28. Claudia Parsons, "NY Play 'Fat Pig' Tackles What May Be the Last Taboo." *Reuters*, http://www.reuters.com, December 25, 2004.

29. There are college courses offered such as Sociology of the Body, taught at City University in New York by Victoria Pitts. Relevant texts useful for educational purposes have been cited throughout this book.

30. Sondra Solovay, *Tipping the Scales of Justice: Fighting Weight-Based Discrimination*. Amherst, NY: Prometheus Books, 2000. See especially p. 237, in which the author finds that size bias has similarities to other biases (sexism, racism, etc.).

31. Debra L. Gimlin, *Body Work: Beauty and Self-Image in American Culture*. Berkeley, CA: University of California, 2002, p. 138.

32. Ibid., p. 131.

33. Bill Finley, "Rider Struggles to Overcome Her Good Looks." *New York Times* (May 18, 2005): A23, A26.

34. Denise Lavoie, "Librarian Sues Harvard over 'Pretty' Bias." *Seattle Post-Intelligencer*, http://www.seattlepi.nwsource.com, March 22, 2005.

35. Peter N. Stearns, *Fat History: Bodies and Beauty in the Modern West*. New York: New York University, 1997, p. viii.

36. Gimlin, *Body Work*, p. 132.

37. Wann, *Fat!So?*

38. Frater, *Fat Chicks Rule*, pp. 92, 108, 111, 114.

39. Ibid., p. 154.

40. Frederic J. Frommer, "Ex-FBI Whistle-Blower Mulls Congress Bid." *Seattle Post-Intelligencer*, http://www.seattlepi.nwsource.com, May 24, 2005. Ms. Rowley ran, unsuccessfully, for the Democratic for a seat in the 2nd Congressional District in Minnesota.

41. Wolf, *The Beauty Myth*, p. 2.

Bibliography

Alexander, Susan M. "Stylish Hard Bodies: Branded Masculinity in *Men's Health* Magazine." *Sociological Perspectives* 46 (2003): 535–554.

Anspaugh, Jean Renfro. *Fat Like Us*. Durham, NC: Windows on History, 2001.

Banet-Weiser, Sarah. *The Most Beautiful Girl in the World: Beauty Pageants and National Identity*. Berkeley, CA: University of California Press, 1999.

Berry, Bonnie. 2004. "The Power of Looks: An Historical Analysis of Social Aesthetics and Status Gain." Presented at the annual meeting of the Society for the Study of Social Problems, August 14, San Francisco, CA.

———. "Animal Aesthetics: Remaking Animals to Suit Our Image." *Animals and Society* 5 (2004): 11–12.

———. 2004. "Social Aesthetics: Public Reaction to Looks." Presented at the Annual Meeting of the Association for Humanist Sociology, November 13, 2004, Louisville, KY.

———. 2005. "Social Aesthetics: Reconstructions of Body Size." Presented at the Annual Meeting of the Society for the Study of Social Problems, August 13, Philadelphia, PA.

Black, Edwin. *War against the Weak: Eugenics and America's Campaign to Create a Master Race*. London: Four Walls Eight Windows, 2003.

Blum, Virginia L. *Flesh Wounds: The Culture of Cosmetic Surgery*. Berkeley, CA: University of California Press, 2003.

Bordo, Susan. "'Material Girl': the Effacement of Postmodern Culture." *Michigan Law Review* 29 (1990): 657.

———. *Unbearable Weight: Feminism, Western Culture and the Body*. Berkeley, CA: University of California Press, 1995.

Bovey, Shelley. *The Forbidden Body*. London: Pandora, 1989.

Braziel, Jana Evans and Kathleen LeBesco (eds.). *Bodies out of Bounds: Fatness and Transgression*. Berkeley, CA: University of California Press, 2001.

Brumberg, Joan Jacobs. *The Body Project: An Intimate History of American Girls*. New York: Vintage Books, 1998.

Burris-Kitchen, Deborah J. *Short Rage: An Autobiographical Look at Heightism in America*. Santa Barbara, CA: Fithian Press, 2002.

Campos, Paul. *The Obesity Myth: Why America's Obsession with Weight is Hazardous to Your Health*. New York: Gotham Books, 2004.

Chernin, Kim. *The Obsession: Reflections on the Tyranny of Slenderness*. New York: Harper and Row, 1981.

Critser, Greg. *Fatland*. Boston, MA: Houghton Mifflin, 2003.

Darwin, Charles. *The Descent of Man and Selection in Relation to Sex*. New York: Routledge, 1871.

deRiencourt, Amaury. *Sex and Power in History*. New York: David McKay, 1974.

Edwards, Korie, Katrina M. Carter-Tellison, and Cedric Herring. 2004. "For Richer, for Poorer: Whether Dark or Light Skin: Skin Tone, Marital Status, and Spouse's Earnings," pp. 65–81 in *Skin/Deep: How Race and Complexion Matter in the "Color-Blind" Era*, edited by C. Herring, V. M. Keith, and H. D. Horton, Chicago, IL: University of Illinois Press.

Etcoff, Nancy. *Survival of the Prettiest: The Science of Beauty*. New York: Anchor Books, 1991.

Finklestein, Joan. *The Fashioned Self*. Philadelphia, PA: Temple University Press, 1991.

Frater, Lara. *Fat Chicks Rule: How to Survive in a Thin-Centric World*. Brooklyn, NY: IG, 2005.

Gilman, Sander L. "Ethnicity and Aesthetic Surgery," pp. 110–135 in *Aesthetic Surgery*, edited by A. Taschen. Koln, Germany: Taschen, 2005.

———. *Making the Body Beautiful: A Cultural History of Aesthetic Surgery*. Princeton, NJ: Princeton University Press, 1999.

Gimlin, Debra L. *Body Work: Beauty and Self Image in American Culture*. Berkeley, CA: University of California Press, 2002.

Goodman, W. Charisse. *The Invisible Woman: Confronting Weight Prejudice in America*. Carlsbad, CA: Gurze, 1995.

Grealey, Lucy. *Autobiography of a Face*. Boston, MA: Houghton Mifflin, 1994.

Hall, Stephen S. *Size Matters: How Height Affects the Health, Happiness, and Success of Boys—and the Men They Become*. New York: Houghton Mifflin, 2006.

Herring, Cedric, Verna M. Keith, and Hayward Derrick Horton (eds.). *Skin/Deep: How Race and Complexion Matter in the "Color-Blind" Era*. Chicago, IL: University of Illinois Press, 2004.

Huff, Joyce L. "A 'Horror of Corpulence': Interrogating Bantingism and Mid-Nineteenth-Century Fat Phobia," pp. 39–59 in *Bodies Out of Bounds: Fatness and Transgression*, edited by J. E. Braziel and K. LeBesco. Berkeley, CA: University of California Press, 2001.

Kaplan, Louise J. *Female Perversions: The Temptations of Emma Bovary*. Northvale, NJ: Jason Aronson, 1997.

Kaw, E. "'Opening' Faces: The Politics of Cosmetic Surgery and Asian American Women," pp. 241–265 in *Many Mirrors: Body Image and Social Relations*, edited by N. Sault. New Brunswick, NJ: Rutgers University Press, 1994.

Kent, Le'a. "Fighting Abjection," pp. 130–150 in *Bodies out of Bounds: Fatness and Transgression*, edited by J. E. Braziel and K. LeBesco. Berkeley, CA: University of California Press, 2001.

Klein, Richard. "Fat Beauty," pp. 19–38 in *Bodies out of Bounds: Fatness and Transgression*, edited by J. E. Braziel and K. LeBesco. Berkeley, CA: University of California Press, 2001.

Longmore, Paul K. *Why I Burned My Book and Other Essays on Disability*. Philadelphia, PA: Temple University Press, 2003.

Manheim, Camryn. *Wake Up, I'm Fat*. New York: Broadway Books, 1999.

Mayer, Vivian. Foreword of *Shadow on a Tightrope: Writings by Women on Fat Oppression*, edited by Lisa Schoenfielder and Barb Weiser. Iowa City, IA: Aunt Lute, 1983.

Mead, George Herbert. *Mind, Self and Society*. Chicago, IL: University of Chicago Press, 1974.

Mosher, Jerry. "Setting Free the Bears: Refiguring Fat Men on Television," pp. 166–193 in *Bodies out of Bounds: Fatness and Transgression*, edited by J. E. Braziel and K. LeBesco. Berkeley, CA: University of California Press, 2001.

Ping, Wang. *Aching for Beauty: Footbinding in China*. Minneapolis, MN: University of Minnesota Press, 2000.

Postrel, Virginia. 2003. "Going to Great Lengths." *New York Times Magazine*, August 13, p. 16.

———. *The Substance of Style*. New York: HarperCollins, 2003.

Reischer, Erica and Kathryn S. Koo. "The Body Beautiful." *Annual Review of Anthropology* 33 (2004): 297–317.

Riordan, Teresa. *Inventing Beauty: A History of the Innovations That Have Made Us Beautiful*. New York: Broadway Books, 2004.

Roehling, Mark V. "Weight-Based Discrimination in Employment: Psychological and Legal Aspects." *Personnel Psychology* 52 (1999): 969–1016.

Schildkrout, Enid. "Inscribing the Body." *Annual Review of Anthropology* 33 (2004): 319–344.

Schwartz, Hillel. *Never Satisfied: A Cultural History of Diets, Fantasies, and Fat*. New York: Free Press, 1986.

Schweik, Susan. *The Ugly Laws*. New York: New York University Press, forthcoming.

Shell, Ellen Ruppel. "New World Syndrome." *The Atlantic Monthly* 287(6) (2001): 50–53.

Solovay, Sondra. *Tipping the Scales of Justice: Fighting Weight-Based Discrimination*. Amherst, NY: Prometheus, 2000.

Sterns, Peter N. *Fat History: Bodies and Beauty in the Modern West.* New York: New York University Press, 1997.

Van Wolputte, Steven. "Hang on to Your Self: Of Bodies, Embodiment, and Selves." *Annual Review of Anthropology* 33 (2004): 251–269.

Veblen, Thorstein. "The Economic Theory of Woman's Dress." *Popular Science Monthly* December (1984): 203.

Wann, Marilyn. *Fat! So?* Berkeley, CA: Ten Speed Press, 1998.

Wolf, Naomi. *The Beauty Myth: How Images of Beauty Are Used against Women.* New York: Harper Perennial, 2002.

Yalom, Marilyn. *A History of the Breast.* New York: Knopf, 1997.

Subject Index

Abercrombie and Fitch, 46, 96
Aesthetic versus reconstructive
    surgery, 73–74
Age and appearance, 37, 47, 68,
    77–78
Airline seating, discrimination, 98–99
Attribution theory, 32–33

Barbie dolls, 59–60
Bariatric surgery. See Gastric by-pass
    surgery
Beauty standards, 2–5
BFOQ (bona fide occupational
    qualification), 52
"Black is beautiful," 6, 76, 123
Bona fide qualification (for
    employment), 47

Capitalism, 12, 26–27, 57, 59, 98,
    105–8. See also Economic forces
CDCP (Centers for Disease Control
    and Prevention), 21–22, 28, 58
Cellulite, 63, 81
Children, attractiveness of, 35–36

Children of size, 23–24
Costs of cosmetic surgery, 72
Costs of cosmetics and cosmeceuticals,
    65
Costs of weight control, 55, 57

Deformities, disfigurements, 4, 10,
    48–49, 119
Dental care, 65–66, 87
Deservingness and choice, 17, 24–26,
    44–45, 90–91
Disability, disabled, 4, 19–20, 44–45,
    88
Disadvantages of beauty, 49–51,
    121–22

Economic forces, esp. profits and
    capitalism, 12, 26–27, 57, 59, 98
Evolutionary forces, 18, 31
Eyelid surgery, 76–77

Face lifts, 77–78, 80
Face transplants, 73
Fashion models, 7, 47, 58, 113

Fat acceptance, 8–9, 12, 44, 107, 116, 118, 123
"Fat admirers," 34
Fat-and-fit perspective, 20–22
"Fat ordinance," 97–98
Food industry, 102–5
Foot beautification surgery, 78–79, 117
Footbinding, 34, 83, 117

Gastric by-pass surgery, 73–74, 92
Gender and age, 96
Gender and cosmetics, esp. men's use, 69–70
Gender and size, 33–34, 39–40, 41, 43, 47, 57, 96–97
Gender and surgery, 75–76
G.I. Joe dolls, 59

Hair color, straightening, and remover, 68–69
Hair transplants, 79–80
Health and size, 6, 88–89, 91–92
Height, 39, 45–46, 60–62, 87–88
Historical, changing standards for appearance, 5–7, 27, 59, 64–65
Homogenization, standardization of appearance, 81–82, 101–2, 115
Humatrope growth hormone, 60–62

Irish nose, 11
ISAA (International Size Acceptance Association), 118

Jewish nose, 11

Leg lengthening surgery, 79
Liposuction, 80–81

Media and appearance, 36–37
Medical treatment, biases against people-of-size, 91–92
Miss America beauty contests, 115
Morality, 6, 21

NAAFA (National Association for the Advancement of Fat Acceptance), 34, 41, 118, 121, 123
Normalization, 17, 28, 114

Obesogenic environments, 24–25

PBQ (professional beauty qualification), 51–52
Penile transplants, 80
Penis enlargement surgery, 80

Race and appearance, 6, 34, 68, 76–77
Rational bias theory, 51
Reconstructive surgery, 73–75

Scarification, 83
Skin color, 34, 66–67
Social Exchange theory, 32–33
Socioeconomics and appearance, 6, 23, 87, 108–9
Solutions to appearance bias, 118–21
Steroid use, 59–60
Subjectivity, 2–5

"Tyranny of skinny," 58

Ugly laws, 3–4, 100, 118–19

"Valid discrimination," 51

Weight standards, 8, 88–89

Name Index

ADA (Americans with Disabilities Act), 44, 48

Alexander, Susan M., 18, 69, 107, 135, 145, 152

Anspaugh, Jean Renfro, 26, 29, 32, 57, 106, 138, 152

Banet-Weiser, Sarah, 20, 110, 136, 153

Berry, Bonnie, 3, 31, 33, 39, 91, 133, 138, 139, 150

Black, Edwin, 93, 116, 150, 154

Blum, Virginia L., 4, 72, 75, 77, 109, 134, 146–47, 152

Bordo, Susan, 18, 68, 83, 115, 135, 145, 148–49, 154

Bovey, Shelley, 27, 137

Braziel, Jana Evans and Kathleen LeBesco, 27, 56, 58, 118, 137, 142, 154

Brumberg, Joan Jacobs, 117, 154

Burris-Kitchen, Deborah J., 62, 143

Campos, Paul, 21, 136

Critser, Greg, 23–24, 26, 28, 56–57, 103-104, 109, 116, 136–37, 141–42, 151–52, 154

Darwin, Charles, 4, 134

EEOC (Equal Employment Opportunity Commission), 48–49

Etcoff, Nancy, 3, 18, 21, 30–31, 33, 35, 40, 46–47, 49–51, 60, 63, 65, 68, 78, 101, 110, 133, 138–41, 143–45, 147, 151, 153

Finklestein, Joan, 83, 149

Frater, Lara, 115, 123, 154–55

Gilman, Sander, L., 4, 6, 11, 72–73, 75–77, 102, 119, 134–35, 146–47, 155

Gimlin, Debra L., 7, 14, 27, 98, 121, 123, 135, 137–38, 150, 155

Goodman, Charisse, 26, 137

Grealey, Lucy, 29, 138

Hall, Stephen, 60, 143
Herring, Cedric, Verna M. Keith, and
 Hayward Derrick Horton, 6, 67,
 134, 145
Huff, Joyce, 27, 88–89, 134, 149

Kaw, E., 77, 147
Klein, Richard, 56, 142

Longmore, Paul, 18–19, 88, 135, 149

Miller, Paul Steven, 45, 62, 96

Ping, Wang, 35–36, 117, 138, 154
Postrel, Virginia, 49, 61–62, 64, 66,
 68, 72, 141, 143–45

Reischer, Erica and Kathryn Koo, 62,
 65, 76, 110, 143–44, 147, 153
Riordan, Teresa, 50, 63–66, 69, 75,
 82, 141, 143–46, 148
Robichaud, Samantha, 48–49
Roehling, Mark, 40–41, 43–44, 51,
 88, 96, 139, 140, 149, 150

Schildkrout, Enid, 67, 145
Schwartz, Hillel, 57, 142
Schweik, Susan, 3, 100, 118–19, 134,
 151, 155
Sheppard, Deborah L., 52
Solovay, Sondra, 9, 41, 43–44, 49, 57,
 90, 108, 121, 135, 139–40, 142,
 149, 152, 155
Stearns, Peter N., 5–6, 8, 21, 34,
 41–42, 57, 89–90, 123, 135,
 138–39, 142, 149, 155

Title VII, 96

Van Wolputte, Steven, 83, 149
Veblen, Thorstein, 50, 68, 141
Voigt, Deborah, 42, 119

Wann, Marilyn, 8, 33, 43, 88–89, 91,
 97, 118, 123, 125, 138, 140,
 149–50, 154, 155
Wolf, Naomi, 2–3, 9, 27, 47–48,
 50–52, 96, 101, 110, 113, 115, 133,
 135, 137, 141, 150–51, 153–54

About the Author

BONNIE BERRY is the Director of the Social Problems Research Group in Gig Harbor, Washington, and formerly university faculty at the University of Miami, University of California at Los Angeles, University of Washington, Indiana University, and Pacific Lutheran University. A sociologist, she is the author of *Social Rage: Emotion and Cultural Conflict* (1999) as well as many journal articles on the topics of social inequality, criminology, and animal rights.